813.54 Tho
Thomas Pynchon

$ 22.95

THOMAS PYNCHON

EDITED AND WITH AN
INTRODUCTION BY HAROLD BLOOM

CURRENTLY AVAILABLE

BLOOM'S MAJOR NOVELISTS

Jane Austen
The Brontës
Willa Cather
Stephen Crane
Don DeLillo
Charles Dickens
Fyodor Dostoevsky
George Eliot
William Faulkner
F. Scott Fitzgerald
Thomas Hardy
Nathaniel Hawthorne
Ernest Hemingway
Henry James
James Joyce
Franz Kafka
D. H. Lawrence
Herman Melville
Toni Morrison
Marcel Proust
Thomas Pynchon
John Steinbeck
Stendhal
Leo Tolstoy
Mark Twain
Alice Walker
Edith Wharton
Virginia Woolf

THOMAS PYNCHON

EDITED AND WITH AN INTRODUCTION
BY HAROLD BLOOM

Philadelphia

© 2003 by Chelsea House Publishers, a subsidiary of
Haights Cross Communications.

A Haights Cross Communications Company

Introduction © 2003 by Harold Bloom.

All rights reserved. No part of this publication may be reproduced
or transmitted in any form or by any means without the written
permission of the publisher.

Printed and bound in the United States of America.

First Printing
1 3 5 7 9 8 6 4 2

Library of Congress Cataloging-in-Publication Data
Thomas Pynchon / edited and with an introduction by Harold Bloom.
    p. cm — (Bloom's major novelists)
Includes index.
   ISBN 0-7910-7030-1
   1. Pynchon, Thomas—Criticism and interpretation. I. Bloom, Harold.
II. Series.
PS3566.Yff Z94 2003
813'.54—dc21

                                                                                   2002155990

Chelsea House Publishers
1974 Sproul Road, Suite 400
Broomall, PA 19008-0914

http://www.chelseahouse.com

Contributing Editor: Dave Kress

Cover design by Terry Mallon

Layout by EJB Publishing Services

CONTENTS

User's Guide	7
About the Editor	8
Editor's Note	9
Introduction	10
Biography of Thomas Pynchon	12
Plot Summary of *The Crying of Lot 49*	15
List of Characters in *The Crying of Lot 49*	21
Critical Views on *The Crying of Lot 49*	23
Anne Mangel on Pynchon's Use of Science and Technology	23
Frank Kermode on the Use of Codes	26
N. Katherine Hayles on the Effects of Ambiguity	28
Gregory Flaxman on Connections between Paranoia and Meaning	33
John W. Hunt on the Intersection of Comedy and Clarity	36
Tony Tanner on the Function of Entropy	41
Plot Summary of *V.*	47
List of Characters in *V.*	53
Critical Views on *V.*	57
Kenneth Kupsch on the True Identity of V.	57
Mark Sanders on the Critique of Traditional History	62
Mark D. Hawthorne on the Creation and Effects of Gender and Gender Roles	65
Melvyn New on the Examination of the Processes of Criticism	68
Deborah L. Madsen on the Elusiveness and Allusiveness of V.	71
Josephine Hendin on the Figure of Death	76
Plot Summary of *Gravity's Rainbow*	81
List of Characters in *Gravity's Rainbow*	88
Critical Views on *Gravity's Rainbow*	91
David Cowart on the Implications of Film and Cinema	91
John Hamill on the Role of Sadomasochism	95
Jeffrey S. Baker on the Radical Critique of American Imperialism in the 1960s	97
Edward Mendelson on Encyclopedic Nature	102

Gabriele Schwab on Confrontation with the Specter of the Unspeakable	106
John O. Stark on the Difficulty for Readers Presented by Scientific and Technical Information	110
Plot Summary of *Mason & Dixon*	116
List of Characters in *Mason & Dixon*	121
Critical Views on *Mason & Dixon*	124
Elizabeth Jane Wall Hinds on the Connections between the 18th and 20th Centuries	124
David Cowart on the Conflict between Rationality and Spirituality	128
Ashton Nichols on the Cultural Importance of Literary Epiphany	133
William Logan on the Connections between Poetry and Fiction	138
William McCarron on the Theme of Separation and Linkage	143
Alessia Ricciardi on Experimental Postmodernity	145
Works by Thomas Pynchon	150
Works about Thomas Pynchon	151
Acknowledgments	155
Index of Themes and Ideas	158

USER'S GUIDE

This volume is designed to present biographical, critical, and bibliographical information on the author and the author's best-known or most important works. Following Harold Bloom's editor's note and introduction is a concise biography of the author that discusses major life events and important literary accomplishments. A critical analysis of each novel follows, tracing significant themes, patterns, and motifs in the work. An annotated list of characters supplies brief information on the main characters in each work.

A selection of critical extracts, derived from previously published material, follows each thematic analysis. In most cases, these extracts represent the best analysis available from a number of leading critics. Because these extracts are derived from previously published material, they will include the original notations and references when available. Each extract is cited, and readers are encouraged to use the original publications as they continue their research. A bibliography of the author's writings, a list of additional books and articles on the author and their work, and an index of themes and ideas conclude the volume.

As with any study guide, this volume is designed as a supplement to the works being discussed, and is in no way intended as a replacement for those works. The reader is advised to read the text prior to using this study guide, and to keep it accessible for quick reference.

ABOUT THE EDITOR

Harold Bloom is Sterling Professor of the Humanities at Yale University and Henry W. and Albert A. Berg Professor of English at the New York University Graduate School. He is the author of over 20 books, and the editor of more than 30 anthologies of literary criticism.

Professor Bloom's works include *Shelley's Mythmaking* (1959), *The Visionary Company* (1961), *Blake's Apocalypse* (1963), *Yeats* (1970), *A Map of Misreading* (1975), *Kabbalah and Criticism* (1975), *Agon: Toward a Theory of Revisionism* (1982), *The American Religion* (1992), *The Western Canon* (1994), and *Omens of Millennium: The Gnosis of Angels, Dreams, and Resurrection* (1996). *The Anxiety of Influence* (1973) sets forth Professor Bloom's provocative theory of the literary relationships between the great writers and their predecessors. His most recent books include *Shakespeare: The Invention of the Human*, a 1998 National Book Award finalist, *How to Read and Why* (2000), and *Genius: A Mosiac of One Hundred Exemplary Creative Minds* (2002).

Professor Bloom earned his Ph.D. from Yale University in 1955 and has served on the Yale faculty since then. He is a 1985 MacArthur Foundation Award recipient and served as the Charles Eliot Norton Professor of Poetry at Harvard University in 1987–88. In 1999 he was awarded the prestigious American Academy of Arts and Letters Gold Medal for Criticism. Professor Bloom is the editor of several other Chelsea House series in literary criticism, including BLOOM'S MAJOR SHORT STORY WRITERS, BLOOM'S MAJOR NOVELISTS, BLOOM'S MAJOR DRAMATISTS, BLOOM'S MODERN CRITICAL INTERPRETATIONS, BLOOM'S MODERN CRITICAL VIEWS, and BLOOM'S BIOCRITIQUES.

EDITOR'S NOTE

My Introduction revisits *The Crying of Lot 49* to ponder the current relation between the paranoia of Oedipa's America and the paranoia of President George W. Bush's America.

I find particularly useful the reflections of the late Tony Tanner on entropy in *The Crying of Lot 49*.

On *V.*, Melvyn New explores what could be called the Sternean element in the novel, while Josephine Hendin broods impressively on the figure of death in the book.

John Hamill trenchantly examines sadomasochism in *Gravity's Rainbow*.

Mason & Dixon is illuminated, for me, by the linkage of the 18th and 20th century by Elizabeth Jane Wall Hinds.

INTRODUCTION
Harold Bloom

I suppose that Pynchon's masterwork, to date, is *Mason & Dixon*, but my personal passion for *The Crying of Lot 49* is too strong to yield to any other book. Visionary romance is the genre of *The Crying of Lot 49*. The book seems like a lot of other things: detective story turned inside out, social satire, American apocalypse, but essentially it is romance, a narrative that so meshes fantasy and American reality that they cannot be disengaged. Its protagonist, Oedipa, is amiable but persuasive neither as personality nor as character. She doesn't have to be. After thirty-six years, *The Crying of Lot 49* is perfectly revelatory of current American paranoia in the Age of George W. Bush.

Since the United States, at this time, looks to me like a disorganized paranoia (though such mighty archons as Ashcroft and Poindexter labor to organize it), one feels that it ought to engender an opposing force like the Tristero, an underground postal system that is something of an alternative culture. There cannot, in our America, be any alternative cultures because Dubya, the entertainment industry, the universities, the media, all have subsumed one another. The Tristero, sublimely paranoid, is too different to be absorbed. It will not go to war with Iraq, it will not vote, it will not pay taxes or postal fees. It is what Pynchon elsewhere terms sado-anarchism.

As such, it is a parody of Pentecostalism; *The Crying of Lot 49* is neither political nor religious in its stance. But it is very concerned with the United States of America: is the Tristero system an anarchist alternative to America? Pynchon answers no questions, but something in Oedipa's final meditation may constitute an implicit answer:

> Another mode of meaning behind the obvious, or none. Either Oedipa in the orbiting ecstasy of a true paranoia, or a real Tristero. For there either was some Tristero beyond the appearance of the legacy America, or there was just America and if there was just America then it seemed the only way she could continue, and manage to be at all relevant to it, was as an alien, unfurrowed, assumed full circle into some paranoia.

This marvelously intricate passage comes down to a grim choice of realities: paranoia or sado-anarchism. I wake up these mornings, drink tea, and stare at (I cannot quite read it) *The New York Times*, which clearly is paranoid. The first page (Monday, November 25, 2002) tells me about a young female evangelist murdered in Lebanon, and imparts the news (which is no news) that the middle class in Dubya's paranoia are losing their health benefits. Further down, there is a story about whether or not women will join a golf club. And so it goes. There had better be a Tristero, at least in our imaginations.

BIOGRAPHY OF
Thomas Pynchon

Because he decided at the start of his writing career that his work should take precedence over his own notability, Pynchon has eschewed nearly all personal attention; as a result, surprisingly little is known about one of the most gifted and cutting-edge authors of the second half of the 20th century. What little information we do have is confined almost solely to his academic career and his jobs until he published his first major works. After that, we know almost nothing of the man except for the books he has written and the reviews of the critics who have read them.

Thomas Ruggles Pynchon, Jr. was born on May 8, 1937 in Glen Cove, New York. His father was Thomas Ruggles Pynchon, Sr. and his mother Katherine Frances Bennett Pynchon; he has a sister, Judith and a brother, John. Pynchon was raised as a Catholic, and at age sixteen, he graduated from high school as the salutatorian of his class and went on to Cornell University to major in Engineering Physics. After his sophomore year, he interrupted his studies to serve two years in the Navy.

Going back to Cornell in 1957, he switched majors to English, taking courses with Vladimir Nabokov, editing the student newspaper, and writing his first short stories. He graduated with honors in 1959 and began to publish much of his short fiction including, "Mortality and Mercy in Vienna," "Lowlands," "Entropy," and "Under the Rose."

At the same time, he started *V.*, his first novel, while working as an engineer in Seattle for Boeing. *V.* was published in 1963 and won the William Faulkner Foundation Award for best first novel of the year. In 1965 Pynchon published in *Esquire* an early version of what was later to become the short novel *The Crying of Lot 49* called "The World (This One), the Flesh (Mrs. Oedipa Maas), and the Testament of Pierce Inverarity." The novel itself was published a year later and won the Richard and Hilda Rosenthal Foundation Award of the National Institute of Arts and Letters.

It was at this time that Pynchon withdrew almost completely

from the public arena, spending the next seven years working on his greatest novel, *Gravity's Rainbow*, which was published in 1973, winning the National Book Award for fiction in 1974. The novel was also selected by the judges of the Pulitzer Prize in literature, but in an unprecedented move, the Pulitzer advisory board invalidated the judges' decision, and no Pulitzer was given for literature in 1974. In 1975 *Gravity's Rainbow* was also awarded the William Dean Howells Medal of the American Academy of Arts and Letters, but Pynchon, perhaps in response to the Pulitzer decision, this time refused to accept the award. Pynchon also received the National Book Award for *Gravity's Rainbow*, but instead of accepting it himself, he sent rhapsodic comedian Irwin Corey to accept it on his behalf.

From this point on, there has been almost no substantive information on Pynchon other than the books and articles he has published. In 1984, a collection of his short stories entitled *Slow Learner* was published; in 1989, he received a John D. and Catherine T. MacArthur Foundation Fellowship; and in 1990 his novel *Vineland* was released. His most recent work of fiction is the novel *Mason & Dixon*, which was published in 1998.

In addition to his fiction, Pynchon has also written several pieces for *The New York Times Magazine*, including "A Journey Into The Mind of Watts," "Is It O.K. To Be A Luddite?" and most recently an essay on sloth.

Over the years, the reclusiveness of Pynchon has itself become a topic of speculation for many fans of the author's. At times people have suggested he is "really" J.D. Salinger, that he is a script writer for the famous "Mystery Science Theater 3000" television show, and that a series of letters written to a local paper in California by a homeless woman named Wanda Tinasky were actually penned by Pynchon. Other theorists suggest that there is no one Pynchon but that he is a series of writers who prefer to remain anonymous, but more credible reports seem to indicate that he simply likes his privacy and leads what amounts to a very sedate and "normal" life. At various times he has lived in California, New York, Boston, London, and in Mexico, but his exact whereabouts and details of his private life remain unknown. Rumors of his addiction to junk food and TV continue to surface

(Pynchon sanctioned the use of his name and one of his characters from *V.* for episodes of *The John Laroquette Show*), as do reported sightings and encounters from around the world, but to this day his private life remains just that, and all we have to go on while discussing his work is the work itself—which is exactly as it should be, according to Pynchon.

PLOT SUMMARY OF
The Crying of Lot 49

Often used as a starting point in Pynchon studies because of its straightforward narrative and almost traditional plot and style, the novel begins as Mrs. Oedipa Maas returns home from a Tupperware party to learn she has been named executrix for the estate of Pierce Inverarity, her former lover. Inverarity, a tycoon who had once lost two million dollars "in his spare time," had last spoken to her a year earlier in a bizarre, middle-of-the-night phone call. Oedipa is married to Wendell "Mucho" Maas, a used car salesman turned disc jockey who is wracked by uncertainty because of the fluctuating ethics of his profession and the erratic course of his life. The next day, Oedipa meets with the couple's lawyer, Roseman, who plays footsie with her while explaining the duties of an executrix. Unsure of why she has been named executrix, and feeling distant and disconnected both from her husband and her day-to-day life, but also curious about what she may find while sorting out the estate, Oedipa sets off to San Narciso—a town in southern California, near Los Angeles—to begin her examination of Inverarity's legacy.

From this simple if humorously ominous beginning, the novel, which shares many qualities with other, earlier California detective novels, soon casts Oedipa into the endless conundrum of America—and perhaps life—itself: which force rules the universe, order or chaos?

In San Narciso, Oedipa drives by Yoyodyne, a huge defense corporation owned in part by Inverarity, and she finally takes a room at the Echo Courts Motel, in part because the nymph on the motel's sign looks so much like her. There, Oedipa meets Miles, the sixteen-year old manager of the motel and member of a faux British band, The Paranoids.

That evening, Inverarity's lawyer, Metzger, comes to the hotel. At first Oedipa thinks that someone—"They"—must be trying to play with her because he is too good-looking to be real: he must, she assumes, be an actor. In fact she is close to the truth, because as it turns out, Metzger had indeed been an actor once—

"Baby Igor," a child star of old movies. Oedipa turns on the television to find one of Metzger's movies. *Cashiered* is its name, and it tells the story of a father, son, and Saint Bernard commando team who prowl the waters around Gallipoli in their miniature submarine sinking Turkish warships.

More convinced than ever that she is being toyed with—all the commercials run during the movie are for companies and/or properties that Inverarity owned—Oedipa makes a bet with Metzger on the movie's ending: with sex as the stakes, Oedipa bets that the crew dies at the end. As the movie progresses, Metzger announces that the reels may be out of order, so the outcome of the film becomes increasingly hard to determine. Oedipa tries to obtain more information on the movie from Metzger, but he agrees to answer questions only if Oedipa takes off one article of clothing for each answer. She in turn agrees, but only after donning an impossible number of layers of additional clothing.

During their ensuing game of "Strip Botticelli," an aerosol can careens around the motel room, the Paranoids drop by for a short visit, and Oedipa and Metzger become increasingly drunk and chaotic. Eventually, they are both naked and begin to have sex. During the course of their love-making, Oedipa falls asleep several times, waking up finally to find herself reaching a sexual climax with Metzger while outside by the pool The Paranoids overload the electrical circuits of the motel with their amplifiers, and the room is blacked out. When the power comes back on Oedipa sees the final moments of the movie: impossibly, given the way that all movies have happy endings, the submarine sinks and father, son, and dog die a horrible death. Metzger tells Oedipa that Inverarity had told him she wouldn't be easy, and even though upon hearing this she begins to cry, they soon return to making love.

The next evening, after receiving a strange letter from Mucho, Oedipa and Metzger travel to a bar called The Scope. The Scope is a haunt of the electronics geeks from the Yoyodyne plant, and there they meet Mike Fallopian, who tells them about the Peter Pinguid Society. Pinguid, a captain in the Confederacy's navy, had sailed around Cape Horn to attack San Francisco and encountered a Russian ship. No real battle took place, but it was commemorated by the Society as the first Russian-American battle.

Fallopian's description of the Society's history and philosophy is cut short by a bizarre "mail call" in the bar. Excusing herself, Oedipa goes to the bathroom where she notices a strange symbol on the wall, a muted horn and the word WASTE. Fallopian explains that the WASTE is an alternate postal system that seeks to both circumvent and also short-circuit the government's monopoly, and he describes a book he is writing as well: the history of private mail delivery in the United States.

Becoming further entangled both in the mystery of Inverarity's will and in a sexual relationship with Metzger, Oedipa joins Metzger and the Paranoids for a picnic at one of Inverarity's properties, Fangoso Lagoons. There they meet one of Metzger's fellow lawyer/actors, Manny Di Presso who is on the run from a client. Stealing a boat, the whole crew travels to an island in the lake where Oedipa learns that Inverarity had received a shipment of bones from Italy for filters of Beaconsfield cigarettes, one of his many companies, but had never paid for them. The bones were the remains of American GIs who had been thrown in a lake after a battle in the Second World War, and when one of the "chicks" who hangs out with The Paranoids hears this, she tells Oedipa that this sounds just like the plot of play by Richard Wharfinger, *The Courier's Tragedy*.

The next day, Oedipa and Metzger go to see the play, which is being performed by the Tank Theatre. It is a complicated tale involving competing postal systems, sex, and violence. During the play, Oedipa hears the word "Tristero" for the first time. Going to speak to Randolph Driblette, the director of the play, in hopes of learning more about the strange coincidences, Oedipa discovers nothing tangible but only more mystery and more overlapping connections.

Oedipa starts to sense that everything will be explained if she can learn more about the Tristero. Deciding to attend a Yoyodyne stockholders' meeting, Oedipa finds herself lost in the huge building. There she meets Stanley Koteks, an engineer who is doodling the WASTE/Tristero muted horn on an envelope.

From Koteks, she learns both that WASTE is not a word but an acronym (W.A.S.T.E.) and of an inventor named John Nefastis who apparently has brought Maxwell's Demon to fruition.

Oedipa learns of a massacre of Wells Fargo men by strangers dressed all in black (also the garb of the Tristero) and begins to see a pattern of sorts emerging in this confusion and chaos. Travelling to San Francisco to find John Nefastis, Oedipa first visits a senior citizen's home Inverarity owned. There she speaks that to a Mr. Thoth whose grandfather had ridden for the Pony Express. Trying to remember the Spanish name of a group of black-feathered "fake Indians," Thoth shows Oedipa a ring of theirs his grandfather took: on it is the muted horn of W.A.S.T.E.

Oedipa also meets Genghis Cohen, who has found something strange in the collection of Inverarity's stamps. Cohen shows her the watermark on a stamp which contains the W.A.S.T.E. horn and some Pony Express stamps which include black feathers and the "misprint," "U.S. Potsage." Oedipa and Cohen realize that the Tristero must still be active after hundreds of years, but Cohen dissuades Oedipa from trying to do anything about it.

In Berkeley, she visits the publisher of Wharfinger's play, and finally obtains a copy of the script. Instead of clearing things up, she finds even more problems in the text. Next, Oedipa finds John Nefastis, who shows her the Demon and explains the concept of entropy and its connection to the transmission of information. She tries to get the Demon to work, but fails and then flees from Nefastis, who wants to have sex with her on the couch with the evening news playing in the background.

It is then that Oedipa begins to see signs of W.A.S.T.E. and the Tristero everywhere: in a gay bar, a man wearing a lapel pin in the shape of the muted horn; in the park, a group of girls stay up all night playing jump rope games with the word "tristoe" in their songs; in a Mexican diner, an anarchist newspaper displays the horn. On a bus and at the airport she sees and hears signs of it. Finally, Oedipa meets an old man tattooed with the horn who asks her to take a letter for his wife to the W.A.S.T.E. drop. Following the W.A.S.T.E. carrier, she finds herself back at Nefastis' house.

Back in her own town, Oedipa has a strange meeting with Dr. Hilarius, her psychiatrist. He is suffering from paranoia because during World War II he experimented on Jews, and as Oedipa approaches his office he begins shooting at anything that moves. Oedipa eventually takes his gun away from him, and upon leaving the office is met and interviewed by Mucho, who is covering the story for his radio station, KCUF. Trying to have a pizza with Mucho, Oedipa realizes that because of Hilarius' experiments with LSD, Mucho has been lost to her—his individual personality splintered into a veritable "chorus."

Oedipa returns to Echo Courts, where she learns that Metzger has run off with one of the Paranoids' fifteen-year-old girlfriends. She also hears from Emory Bortz, the author of the introduction to Wharfinger's play, who invites her to party at his home. When Oedipa asks him about the Tristero, Bortz tells her that the Vatican might be somehow involved with the Tristero and that Driblette has drowned himself: this party is in fact Driblette's wake.

At this point all the threads in Oedipa's quest begin to come apart, and as readers we begin to wonder if she is indeed following something real or making it all up in her mind: has she actually stumbled upon a centuries-old conspiracy or is she mad? But even if the Tristero is "real," is it authentically real or is it a production of Inverarity's, staged somehow for her to stumble upon, to haunt her from beyond the grave? From here, any new information she collects seems tepid and bleak. Cohen informs her that he has found a stamp with an imprint that explains the W.A.S.T.E. acronym, "We Await Silent Tristero's Empire," which may be another clue to the mystery, but she also discovers that Inverarity also owned the Tank Theatre and Zapf's Bookstore—where she purchased the copy of the play.

From Cohen she finally learns that Inverarity's stamps are to be sold at auction as Lot 49. An anonymous bidder has arranged to secure the stamps in absentia, but when Oedipa calls the bidder's agent, she learns that he will appear in the flesh at the auction.

Arriving at the auction she meets Cohen, who is also bidding on the stamps. Inside, Oedipa sits quietly waiting for the "crying" of the auction, wondering what she will do when the mysterious bidder appears. She finds that she truly *knows* nothing, only that she will have to cause some kind of scene and somehow get the authorities involved. At the end of the novel, Oedipa sits alone at the back of the auction room waiting and thinking.

LIST OF CHARACTERS IN
The Crying of Lot 49

The main character and driving force in the story, **Oedipa Maas** is at the start of the novel an ordinary housewife in California. As she follows the trail left behind by Pierce Inverarity in his will, Oedipa leaves behind her day-to-day life as well as her sense of reality. Intelligent, curious, comic, and suspicious, she finds herself unable to sort out the mystery and unable as well to differentiate between reality and appearances, between madness and sanity.

Metzger is a lawyer and former child movie star who has been named as co-executor of the will. Too good-looking to be real, an intense drinker and philanderer, but also the voice of reason or logic in Oedipa's chaotic circle of acquaintances, Metzger has a running affair with Oedipa but in the end leaves her for a fifteen-year-old girl.

Mucho Maas is Oedipa's husband, a former used-car salesman and current disc jockey at station KCUF. He is troubled by the ethics—or lack of them—in his profession, but he also has several affairs with high school girls. Unable to communicate effectively with Oedipa even during the best of times, he joins Dr. Hilarius' LSD experiment and loses all touch with reality.

A California real estate tycoon with whom Oedipa once had an affair, **Pierce Inverarity** is not strictly speaking a character in the novel. Never present as himself except in quirky flashbacks and remembrances, Inverarity nevertheless looms over the entire novel, casting his shadow over all of Oedipa's movements, perhaps directing her as if she were a puppet on a string.

Mike Fallopian is a member of the Peter Pinguid Society who meets Oedipa at The Scope. He informs her about the WASTE system and is quite interested in her search.

Randolph Driblette, director of and actor in *The Courier's Tragedy*, informs Oedipa that the play is sheer entertainment and has no deeper meaning or historical significance. He later commits an apparent suicide by walking into the ocean, but Oedipa suspects it may not have been suicide but rather the work of the Tristero.

The inventor of Maxwell's Demon, **John Nefastis** lets Oedipa try his machine and suggests sex with her when she fails. An expert in entropy, thermodynamics, and information theory, he is also both addicted to and sexually aroused by television.

Philatelist **Genghis Cohen** investigates Inverarity's stamp collection, finding problems and forgeries. Though he seems uninterested in Oedipa's quest, he also finds increasing numbers of clues in the stamps himself.

Doctor Hilarius is both Oedipa and Mucho's psychiatrist. He suffers from guilt and paranoia because of his experiments on Jewish prisoners at Buchenwald, but he is also experimenting with the effects of LSD on housewives and their husbands.

Oedipa's lawyer **Roseman** is another character wracked by paranoia: in his case he is obsessed with television's Perry Mason and with Oedipa. He flirts with her and asks her to run off with him, but when she asks "where to?" he drops the subject entirely.

The sixteen-year-old manager of the Echo Courts Motel, **Miles** is a member of the Paranoids, a high school dropout, and a Peeping Tom during the sexual exploits of Oedipa and Metzger.

CRITICAL VIEWS ON
The Crying of Lot 49

ANNE MANGEL ON PYNCHON'S USE OF SCIENCE AND TECHNOLOGY

> [Anne Mangel wrote this essay as a graduate student at the University of Illinois. Here, she interprets the novel in terms of the influence of science and technology on Pynchon, especially in Pynchon's use of information theory and thermodynamics.]

Like Maxwell's Demon, Oedipa (...) tries to link occurrences, to establish a point of order in what seems to be a random system of information. She vows to be "the dark machine in the centre of the planetarium, to bring the estate into pulsing stelliferous Meaning" (81/58). Her desire to bring order to the mass of confusing interests left by Inverarity leads her to the discovery of "Tristero," a mysterious organization involving a bizarre underground mail system called WASTE. Oedipa sets out to discover the nature and extent of WASTE and Tristero, an obsessive hunt which takes her all over Southern California. Just as the Demon, by sorting the molecules, gains information about them, so Oedipa shuffles through countless people and places, gathering information about the elusive Tristero.

Whatever concrete information Oedipa gains, though, is offset by increasing confusion. The Demon's sorting process can theoretically create a "perpetual motion" machine, and such a machine seems to be operating metaphorically in Oedipa's situation. The clues she gathers yield more clues in an infinite process. Opening out into more and more suggestions, they yield no conclusion. Oedipa gradually senses this. Pondering the information gained from watching *The Courier's Tragedy*, a Jacobean revenge play which contains references to the Tristero, she realizes "these follow-ups were no more disquieting than other revelations which now seemed to come crowding in exponentially, as if the more she collected the more would come to her" (81/58). With her suspicion that the clues are unlimited comes a realization that they will never yield a stelliferous Meaning. She begins to consider whether "the gemlike 'clues' were only some kind of compensation. To make up for her having lost the direct, epileptic Word, the cry that might abolish the night" (118/97).

The parallels between Oedipa and the Demon seem almost too neat. Oedipa painfully discovers that symbols, such as WASTE and its emblem, the muted post horn, do not lead to one stelliferous Meaning. Rather, they point in a thousand different directions and never lead to a solid conclusion. This notion of symbol and metaphor seems to lie at the center of Pynchon's fiction. This idea forms the basis for Pynchon's novel *V.*, where the symbol V. mockingly suggests a chaotic host of irreconcilable things.... Pynchon fashions the Demon metaphor in *The Crying of Lot 49* in a similar way by manipulating it to point in opposite directions. Oedipa does indeed parallel the Demon problem as Maxwell stated it, but paradoxically she also incorporates its opposite, that is, the solution to the Demon dilemma.

The Demon poses a curious problem, partially because it challenges the realm of thermodynamics with a paradox. Since Maxwell introduced the Demon, several scientists have offered solutions to the Demon paradox. Leo Szilard, a physicist, suggested in 1929 that "any action resulting in a decrease in the entropy of a system must be preceded by an operation of acquiring information, which in turn is coupled with the production of an equal or greater amount of entropy." Szilard's idea that the Demon could not actually decrease the net entropy of the system, as Maxwell had supposed, was supported by another physicist, Leon Brillouin, who in 1951 wrote that "an intelligent being, whatever its size, has to cause an increase of entropy before it can effect a reduction by a smaller amount." The innovative idea in Brillouin's solution to the Demon paradox lay in his emphasis on *perception* as increasing the entropy of the system. (...)

The redundancy, irrelevance, ambiguity, and sheer waste involved in language glare from every page of *The Crying of Lot*

49. The one thing Pierce Inverarity transmits, besides his business assets, is an impression of waste in language. His last phone call to Oedipa presents her with "a voice beginning in heavy Slavic tones as second secretary at the Transylvanian Consulate, looking for an escaped bat; modulated to comic-Negro, then on into hostile Pachuco dialect, full of chingas and maricones; then a Gestapo officer asking her in shrieks did she have relatives in Germany and finally his Lamont Cranston voice" (11/2–3). He then assaults Oedipa with the tale of an "old man in the fun house" who was killed by the same gun that killed Professor Quackenbush. "Or something," Oedipa thinks, as if she couldn't really remember the story Inverarity had told and that it didn't matter anyway.... The "or something" phrase insidiously negates the tenuous words which are spoken, is if the information is inaccurate or irrelevant.... The circuitous tales in the novel might be taken as examples of waste and irrelevance in language, but through them, Pynchon is able to incorporate into his own method and style the notions about language he is trying to convey.

The notions involved in Maxwell's Demon, entropy, and information theory reveal a great deal about what Pynchon is doing. By building his fiction on the concept of entropy, or disorder, and by flaunting the irrelevance, redundancy, disorganization, and waste involved in language, Pynchon radically separates himself from earlier twentieth-century writers, like Yeats, Eliot, and Joyce. Thinking of literature in terms of order, rather than disorder, they saw art as perhaps the last way to impose order on a chaotic world. Yet the complex, symbolic structures they created to encircle chaotic experience often resulted in the kinds of static, closed systems Pynchon is so wary of. Pynchon's use of scientific concepts and disorder in his fiction holds a dual excitement, for not only does it sever him from a previous, more rigid and static kind of writing, but it also links him with contemporary artists working in other media who incorporate scientific ideas and seek randomness in their art.

—Anne, Mangel, "Maxwell's Demon, Entropy, Information: *The Crying of Lot 49.*" *Mindful Pleasures: Essays On Thomas Pynchon*, edited by George Levine and David Leverenz, (Boston: Little, Brown and Company, 1976): 90–91, 98–99.

Frank Kermode on the Use of Codes

[Frank Kermode was a Professor of English at Columbia University. He is the author of numerous critical essays and books, including *The Genesis of Secrecy*, *The Sense of an Ending*, and *Not Entitled*. In this essay he discusses the impossibility of reaching a final reading of Pynchon's novel because of the numerous codes its uses to transit its information.]

In *The Crying of Lot 49*, Pynchon's Oedipa, as her name implies, is also confronted with riddles and with the obligation to discover an order. The origin of these riddles is in doubt; it may be the nature of the human world, viewable as waste or as system; it may be a man called Inverarity, who in turn may be either untruth or *dans le vrai*. The book is crammed with disappointed promises of significance, with ambiguous invitations to paradigmatic construction, and this is precisely Oedipa's problem. Is there a structure *au fond*, or only deceptive galaxies of signifiers? Like California itself, the text offers a choice: plenitude or vacuity. Is there a hidden plot concerning an almost Manichaean conflict, which makes sense, whether evil or benign, of the randomness of the world?

Consider the opening: we find Oedipa returning from a Tupperware party; I understand that on these occasions goods are sold outside the normal commercial system. She stands in her living room before a blank television set (communication system without message) and considers the randomness she projects on the world: thoughts about God, a Mexican hotel, dawn at Cornell, a tune from Bartok, a Vivaldi concerto for kazoo. Soon we hear about the coded voices of Inverarity, the culinary Jumble of a Southern California supermarket, her husband's life as a used-car salesman, systematizing, giving meaning to, the trash in old cars. Now he works on a pop radio station, the communication system—without content—of another culture. Later he will start *listening* to Muzak, another type of the empty system. In a world where the psychiatrists provide material for paranoid fantasies, and lawyers are locked in imaginary rivalries with Perry Mason, everybody is tending toward his own dissident universe of meaning; Oedipa is Rapunzel, her own reality let down like hair from her head. Minority cultures, bricolaged from pop, old movies, astrology, coexist in a world whose significances, if any, relate to no conceivable armature.

But Oedipa has "all manner of revelations," and a shadowy armature seems to be taking shape. Is she still in her head, or is the great plot real? If so, is it malign? To discover it may be the same thing as inventing it. What Peter Berger and Thomas Luckmann call "the social construction of reality" proceeds because there are phenomena we cannot simply wish away; death is one, but there are others. The construction is what our social situation permits—say, the national limits, the limits of California, ultimately the limits of dissident groups and our protestant selves. As we plot against reality we comply with or deviate from the institutionalized plots; a great deviation is called a sect if shared, paranoia if not. There is always a way of coding the material, even that which on other views is simply waste. Having instituted a system one keeps it intact either by legitimating extraneous material or, if that is too difficult, or the threat too great, by nihilating it.

Making sense of other somewhat arbitrary symbolic universes, understanding their construction, is an activity familiar to all critics. Certainly it involves choices, a limitation of pluralities. The activity of the critic, thus understood, is nomic. It seeks order, and is analogous to the social construction of reality. What Oedipa is doing is very like reading a book. Of course books can be read in very strange ways—a man once undertook to demonstrate infallibly to me that *Wuthering Heights* was an interlinear gloss on Genesis. How could this be disproved? He had hit on a code, and legitimated all the signs. Oedipa is afraid she may be like that man, or that she is drifting into paranoia, the normal hermeneutic activity in disease, and Pynchon's great subject.

—Frank Kermode, "The Use of Codes in *The Crying of Lot 49.*" *Thomas Pynchon: Modern Critical Views*, edited by Harold Bloom, (New York: Chelsea House Publishers, 1986): 11–12.

N. Katherine Hayles on the Effects of Ambiguity

[N. Katherine Hayles is a Professor of English at the University of California, Los Angeles. Having written extensively on the connections between science and literature, her books include *Chaos Bound: Orderly Disorder in Contemporary Literature and Science*; *Chaos and Order: Complex Dynamics in Literature and Science*; and *How We Became Posthuman: Virtual Bodies in Cybernetics, Literature and Informatics*. In this article, Hayles claims that ambiguity itself in the novel shifts between a view of reality as constructed and views of reality as given, and it is this shift that in turn drives the novel's plot.]

NEARLY everyone who has written about *The Crying of Lot 49* has commented on the ambiguous ending. A sense of mystery or irresolution hangs over the novel even after one has read and reread it many times. Many readers take the lingering ambiguities to signal that *The Crying of Lot 49* is a postmodern text, more interested in revealing the constructed nature of consensual reality than in mimetically reflecting a world that exists independent of our perceptions.[1] Yet as the novel draws to a close there is also a growing sense of limitation, as if Oedipa were coming up against irreducible constraints that limit interpretation and circumscribe action.[2] It may be, then, that the underlying ambiguity of the novel rests between a postmodern view that renders irrelevant the distinctions between life and art, and a realism that reaches beyond construction toward a reality that exists whether or not we apprehend it.[3]

The challenge is to understand how such an ambiguity can be constructed and maintained in a work which exists as a verbal construction, acknowledges itself as such, and yet points beyond to something outside the realm of language. My approach will be through metaphor. To say that something is metaphoric is to imply that it is not literal but a similitude constructed through language. A strict constructivist position maintains that everything is metaphor, since in this view whatever we can speak or know is always already a representation, not reality as such. Yet to say that something is metaphoric is also to evoke the possibility of literal speech, since metaphor is a concept constructed through its difference from literal signification. Metaphor thus paradoxically provides a way to think about the literal and the metaphoric at the same time.

If one were to construct a metaphor that alluded to the literality hidden in the concept of metaphor, one would have a metaphor that was both self-reflexive (that is, referring to a class that includes itself as a member) and self-deconstructing (since by necessity it reveals its own hidden complement of literality). Metaphors that work on this double level I will call meta-metaphors.[4] The self-reflexive and self-deconstructive looping of meta-metaphors is essential to *The Crying of Lot 49*'s construction of its haunting ambiguities. Frank Palmeri made essentially the same point when he argued that *The Crying of Lot 49* can be understood as an attempt to construct a mode of representation that eludes the dichotomy between literal and metaphoric speech.[5] I believe that he is correct, although I want to take the argument in a different direction by referring to the important work on metaphor of Lakoff and Johnson in *Metaphors We Live By*.[6] Bear with me, then, as we take a detour through metaphor seen as the means by which we construct our world.

Lakoff and Johnson make a strong argument for a constructivist understanding of metaphor by demonstrating that so-called "dead" metaphors are very much alive, working to structure thought, direct action, and evoke emotion. As an example, they instance "argument is war."[7] The expression's martial thrust is reinscribed in the language we use to characterize arguments: strategies are planned, positions attacked or defended, claims demolished or established. Such language creates a conceptual framework that profoundly affects how we talk about argument, think about it, and how we actually argue. With war as the governing metaphor, argument is constructed as an activity that has winners and losers. Even relatively congenial arguments often become competitions governed by the desire to win. How different the situation would be, they suggest, if the governing metaphor were "argument is dance." Then the activity would be seen as a collaboration between partners rather than a competition, leading to very different behavior and emotions. The example illustrates that ordinary metaphors such as "argument is war" are not inevitable. They are cultural constructs, expressing the implicit values of the society that produces and is produced by them.

This approach to metaphor has more power than may at first appear. It can be extended to explain why certain expressions and not others appear in a language. Consider the expression "I am up for the party." Lakoff and Johnson demonstrate that it is part of a cluster of phrases implying "up is good."[8] Another cluster of terms implies "front is good." An expression like "upfront" is possible because the values expressed by these two metaphoric clusters are coherent. "Downfront" or "upback" would not work in the same way because the values implicit in these expressions do not easily mesh. The joining of one cluster of values to another is an extension of how metaphors work in general. Metaphors map one set of experiences onto another, making it possible for us to understand each in terms of the other. Ordinary metaphors typically link a physically immediate action or sensation with a more abstract notion. If I say, "I am up for the party," I am comparing a complex emotional state with a spatial orientation grounded in everyday experience. If both parts of a metaphoric comparison were equally abstract, the metaphor would lose its anchor in immediate physical reality and thus much of its force. If both parts were equally immediate, the metaphor would be redundant.

Metaphoric coherence should not be confused with congruence. The joining of one cluster to another, like the mapping of a single concept onto another, is never an exact transposition. Some parts fit, others do not. Just as the "argument is war" metaphor hides the collaborative aspect of argument, so "upfront" hides the fact that holding back and lying low may be more appropriate strategies for some situations. Metaphors do not describe an objective reality, unmediated by a human perspective; rather, they help to construct the world in which we move. This does not mean that they should be avoided. Indeed it would be almost impossible to avoid them, for they are essential to human comprehension. How do we understand reality, except to compare one thing to another? Even seemingly objective measurements are comparisons that have metaphoric roots. If I say a room is five yards wide, for example, I am comparing it to a unit of measure representing the average length of an Anglo-Saxon girdle.[9] If I say the diameter of an atom is 8.34 angstroms, the basis for the comparison has changed, but there is still a comparison at the heart of the statement. Ordinary metaphors involve more elaborate structures than simple measurements, but they are like them in being comparisons. Any comparison, from a measurement of length to a highly wrought trope, suppresses some aspects of a phenomenon in order to bring others into view. Metaphors thus conceal as well as reveal, deconstructing some aspects of experience at the same time that they construct others. (...)

The argument I have pursued here, that the ambiguities preventing any clear-cut resolution of *The Crying of Lot 49* have a coherent structure of expansion and reduction, should not be confused with the claim that the text is logically consistent throughout. I use coherence in Lakoff and Johnson's sense—a structure that allows for slippages as well as for connection, for mappings that never exactly coincide, for comparisons that partially fit and partially do not. In my view, there really is a mystery to *The Crying of Lot 49*. The text cannot quite make up its mind whether its "verbally graceful" metaphors can reach a reality beyond language, and more fundamentally, cannot resolve whether the endeavor to do so is insane or inspired, divine or demonic. Thus the values assigned to the Tristero, keep changing—sometimes menacing, sometimes comforting; sometimes metaphysical abstraction, sometimes historical conspiracy; sometimes illusory, sometimes real. Underlying these uncertainties is the profoundly ambiguous relationship of the text to its own language. Interrogating the conditions of possibility for its utterances, it is never able to resolve whether its language play is a postmodern excursion into consensual constructions or a thrust through the theater curtain to a higher order of reality, in which we may, after all, be mere playthings.

Either possibility has its chances for joy and despair, grief and liberation. The only unthinkable option is not to question, to remain insulated within placid acceptances.

NOTES

1. For a reading of the ambiguous ending that connects it to the new physics, see Lance Olsen, "Pynchon's New Nature: The Uncertainty Principle in *The Crying of Lot 49*," *Canadian Review of American Studies* 14 (1983): 153–63. John P. Leland in "Pynchon's Linguistic Demon: *The Crying of Lot 49*," *Critique* 16 (1974): 45–53, exemplifies a postmodern reading of the novel. A more moderate position is taken by Robert Merrill in "The Form and Meaning of Pynchon's *The Crying of Lot 49*," *Ariel* 8 (1977): 53–71; Merrill argues for strong structural elements along with a postrealistic form.

2. This aspect of the novel has been noticed by many, including Robert Murray Davis in "Parody, Paranoia, and the Dead End of Language in *The Crying of Lot 49*," *Genre* 5 (1972): 367–77.

3. Frank Palmeri makes a similar point in "Neither Literally Nor as Metaphor: Pynchon's *The Crying of Lot 49* and the Structure of Scientific Revolutions," *ELH* 54 (1987): 979–99.

4. I am indebted to conversations with Nancy Barta Smith for these ideas about the literal and the metaphoric, and especially for the term "meta-metaphor."

5. Palmeri, "Neither Literally Nor as Metaphor." Palmeri sees *The Crying of Lot 49* as a paradigm-breaking text, working through a series of models that it deconstructs by proving their constitutive terms inadequate. Among the frames Palmeri considers are information theory and thermodynamics, narcissism, and genre.

6. George Lakoff and Mark Johnson, *Metaphors We Live By* (Chicago: University of Chicago Press, 1980).

7. Ibid., pp. 3–6.

8. Ibid., pp. 14–21.

9. I am indebted for this example, and for the point about the metaphoric basis of measurement, to F. C. McGrath's unpublished manuscript, "How Metaphor Works: What Boyle's Law and Shakespeare's 73rd Sonnet Have in Common."

> —N. Katherine Hayles, "'A Metaphor of God Knew Many Parts': The Engine that Drives *The Crying of Lot 49*." *New Essays on* The Crying of Lot 49, edited by Patrick O'Donnell, (Cambridge: Cambridge UP, 1991): 97–100, 121–122.

Gregory Flaxman on Connections between Paranoia and Meaning

[Gregory Flaxman teaches film theory at the University of Pennsylvania in the Department of English. He is the editor of *The Brain is the Screen: Gilles Deleuze and the Philosophy of Cinema*. In this essay he proposes that Oedipa's paranoia demonstrates a reformulation of Reason from certainty to uncertainty.]

Near the end of *The Crying of Lot 49*, Oedipa Maas finds herself trapped in a stultifying "symmetry of choices" (181). In the process of executing her ex-lover's will, she has seemingly stumbled upon the Tristero, a secret, perhaps anarchic, organization. But is the Tristero the sublime thread which might lead Oedipa out of her own suburban inertia, even out of the hopelessness of her America? Or is the Tristero instead the thread of an idea with which she weaves a sublime delusion? As Oedipa reflects, "Behind the hieroglyphic streets there would either be a transcendent meaning, or only the earth" (181). Indeed, this binary system is readily acknowledged, even thematized, in Pynchon's novel, but the suppositions which ground the duality are not so clear. Ostensibly, discovering the Tristero *qua* reality would be tantamount to the validation of meaning, while acknowledging the delusion of meaning (which Oedipa considers paranoid) would be the acceptance of meaninglessness. But if, at the level of its expression, paranoia is so quantified as to suggest its impossibility, then perhaps that implicit denial conceals another possibility: might an originary paranoiac crisis have brought the symmetry—meaning or meaninglessness—to bear? (...)

Oedipa not only fails to find the Word, but eventually recognizes the dangers that might have befallen if she had found it. Perhaps her dim understanding expresses a retreat from the Thing. Indeed, if we take the text as an intersection of lines—

subjective and exterior—we might also suggest that those lines, having crossed, continue off into space. Once Oedipa leaves San Francisco, the Tristero's multiplicity of references begins to recede almost as if extimacy were being reconstituted. In a sense, it is, for soon we see that, while there may be a number of paranoids in the novel, Oedipa is not (or is no longer) one of them. In fact, her retreat from the Thing coincides with her discovery of madness in others. She stops in Kinneret on her way back to San Narciso, hoping Dr. Hilarius can provide a diagnosis that will explain away the Tristero, relieve her of worrying about it as reality. Instead, she finds Dr. Hilarius himself frightfully paranoid, armed, taking potshots from his office at passing strangers. Worse, once Hilarius has been hauled off by the police, Oedipa finds her own husband horribly deluded. Mucho has been inducted into Hilarius's LSD experiment, and now he lays claim to a pure linguistics, an ability to reduce speech or any tonality to "'pure sound'" (144). The upshot, reports Mucho, is that "'Everybody who says the same words is the same person if the power spectra are the same'" (142). The down side, Oedipa discovers, is that the edges of Mucho's ego have been worn away: Mucho may, at some level, groove with everyone, but at a subjective level, he is no one. Oedipa is dismayed, but her dismay pinpoints a significant change: once she passes the point of intersection, thereby distancing herself from that overwhelming encounter with deadly *jouissance*, representations of consensuality are no longer so idealized. Mucho provides a sobering antipode to Arrabal's anarchist miracle: he purchases the "soul's talent for consensus" with the loss of identity.

Though Oedipa continues to search for the Tristero, she increasingly undertakes to search on different ground. Enlisting a new ally, Professor Emory Bortz, an expert on *The Courier's Tragedy* and a strict textualist, Oedipa signals a return to the signifier and symbolic order. Correlative with this shift, Oedipa becomes "anxious that her revelation not expand beyond a certain point. Lest, possibly, it grow larger than she and assume her to itself" (166). The revelations of the Word no longer exert the same centripetal pull, the promise of metalanguage—an Other of the Other, that is, an Other responsible for the workings of the symbolic order—gradually slackening. For instance, in San Narciso again, Oedipa warily returns to the site of her first premonitions about the Tristero. At the Scope, she scopes out Mike Fallopian, the inveterate right-winger who first laid down the Tristero's prohibition. Oedipa reports the sum of her adventures, but instead of suggesting new avenues of inquiry, Fallopian raises the most perverse possibility: "'Has it ever occurred to you, Oedipa, that somebody's putting you on? That this is all a hoax, maybe something Inverarity set up before he died?'" (167). The notion of such a grandiose plot thrusts Pierce, even though or maybe because he is dead, into the potential role of Other of the Other. Is it possible that Pierce's perverse humor has outlived him, that this escapade is really his will?

A number of references seem to suggest as much, to the reader as well as to Oedipa. A portion of the novel published in *Esquire* bore the title "The World (This One), the Flesh (Mrs. Oedipa Maas), and the Testament of Pierce Inverarity." By the logic of this title's sequence, Pierce would seem to be a devil—a signifying devil who screws with representation (Tanner 57). This devilish Pierce superficially recalls the Cartesian demon who potentially controls the world of appearances. But whereas Descartes's demon causes the philosopher to doubt reality, the devilish Pierce potentially explains symbolic distortions and discrepancies. In this same vein and even more tempting is the notion of Pierce as Oedipa's textual foe. If we take Oedipa to be a kind of detective—her name, as Tony Tanner points out, recalls the original detective, Oedipus (60)—might not Inverarity's name recall Moriarity, Sherlock Holmes's archenemy? The possibility lodged in the reference is clarified by our understanding that Moriarity is not just any criminal, but one whose brilliance and persistent malevolence serve to explain any and all symbolic distortion as deception.

Still, as Oedipa rejects Fallopian's suggestion only to place it scrupulously among other possibilities to explain—or explain away—the Tristero, an implicit doubt remains. Oedipa theorizes that the Tristero must be either a) a reality which represents "a real alternative to the exitlessness"; or b) the hallucination of such an alternative; or c) Pierce's perverse, "grandiose practical joke"; or d) the fantasy of such a plot (170–71). These possibilities ultimately yield her the choice between "[o]nes and zeroes" (182)—meaning and meaninglessness. But, while the duality was previously a permutation of unbelief, it is consummated here as the conscious source of Oedipa's certainty: the unbelief is transformed into a belief in not believing.

The conceptual reconciliation is clarified as the novel comes to a close. Among Pierce's assets, "the Tristero 'forgeries'" (175) in his stamp collection may provide an answer to the Tristero's mystery. The forgeries are to be auctioned as lot 49, and the philatelist Genghis Cohen tells Oedipa that a book bidder who does not wish his identity known has been refused permission to examine those stamps ahead of time. Because the bidder may show up at the auction in person, an answer to the mystery may be at hand. But the novel does not conclude with an identification; rather, it ends with Oedipa anticipating the start of the auction: the "crying" is deferred. Instead of settling on a theory, on meaning, Oedipa "settled back, to await the crying of lot 49" (183). The phrase conceals a final contradiction of Lacanian proportions. As Lacan repeatedly asserts, the psychoanalytic discovery demands the reformulation of reason and the subject: "I am not wherever I am the plaything of my thought; I think of what I am wherever I do not think I am thinking" (Écrits 166). In the same spirit, Oedipa realizes, at the novel's end, that the only possible certainty is the certainty of waiting and, at the limits of that horizon, the certainty of doubt. No longer invested in intentionality, Oedipa invests meaning in the uncertainty of Cartesian aporia. Her desire to know remains, though the fantasy of what might be known is, in a word, pierced.

—Gregory Flaxman, "Oedipa Crisis: Paranoia and Prohibition in *The Crying of Lot 49*." *Pynchon Notes* 40–41 (1997): 41, 56–58.

JOHN W. HUNT ON THE INTERSECTION OF COMEDY AND CLARITY

[John W. Hunt was a Professor of English at Earlham College and the author of *William Faulkner: Art in*

Theological Tension. In this essay Hunt suggests that Pynchon uses comedy in *Lot 49* not satirically to provide a new, alternative, or clearer perception of "truth," but rather to obscure the truth as a whole from his own characters.]

Thomas Pynchon's *V.* and *The Crying of Lot 49* are ... like *Catch-22*, novels in which an ultimate vision is forced from extreme situations and issues in various strategies of comic escape. Yet there the fundamental similarities end. For what is *seen in* Pynchon's novels is deliberately obscured rather than illuminated by the comic elements. Heller, one feels, has something to say and, in his own mode, makes it as clear as he can. Pynchon, one feels on the other hand, has something he is willing only tentatively to suggest, since the connections he sees mean too much if they are really there. Perhaps, his novels plead in desperation, we are wrong about it all. And it is in the way he goes about rendering his theme that Pynchon shows himself to be unusually inventive in technique, even if not wholly successful. For though his first two books are novels of quest for meaning, in each Pynchon has employed methods calculated to defeat his characters *lest* they succeed in seeing too clearly. We have had the novel of the anti-hero before; Pynchon has given us a form for the comic novel of anti-vision. (...)

One can trace in *The Crying of Lot 49* the same anti-vision and the same ambivalence within the questing character which distinguish *V.*, but its plot takes a different turn, for its questing character does make the connections and discover their meaning, though here a full disclosure is withheld from the reader. The angle of developing vision is always that of Oedipa Maas. But she herself is endowed with a lightness of touch, a humorous self-critical disposition, a *joie de vivre*, which saves her almost to the last from the insanity she comes desperately to hope explains the connections she sees. Not many characters on the last page of their story, awaiting final judgment, could whisper to their possible Enemy, "Your fly is open!"

It is in a strangely whimsical vein that the object of Oedipa's quest is conceived, the fantastic cabal of the Tristero system, a vast three-and-a-half-century-old private postal network, patronized now only by solitaries and social outcasts who live outside "the life of the Republic."[2] What sets her off on the quest is a responsibility imposed on her by her dead lover Inverarity to administer his estate. In one of the novel's controlling images, Oedipa thinks of herself as a Rapunzel-like character, encapsulated in a tower. While Inverarity was alive she had remained safe in her tower, knowing that the price she paid was "an absence of an intensity" (p. 20) about life, a lack of surprise. At points and moments she had been aware of the narrowness of her prison; she knew she had settled for such a life because of "gut fear" (p. 21) that outside the tower was only void, only death, or what would pass for it—meanings which would destroy the limited sense she had made of life. Inverarity's will forces her out of the tower and into the void, to face whatever nameless and malignant magic had held her prisoner. Thus, in form, *Lot 49* is, like the Stencil narrative of *V.*, inquisitive, a cosmic detective story alternating between epistemology—how do I know what the facts are?—and metaphysics—what do these facts mean?

Oedipa responds in the spirit of a caper to early intimations that the Tristero exists. The Tristero is a sort of lewd dancer, a stripteaser on the stage of history, and she, in uncovering it, is attempting to see through "The breakaway gowns, net bras, jeweled garters and G-strings of historical figuration." Yet from the beginning she also wonders if what she is after is going to get her in too deeply: when its dance ends, when Tristero's "terrible nakedness" is revealed, would it "come back down the runway, ... bend to her alone among the desolate rows of seats and begin to speak words she never wanted to hear?" (p. 54).

Early in her inquiry into Inverarity's estate she experiences an "odd, religious instant," as she looks at the printed circuit board pattern made by the streets of San Narciso, the headquarters of Inverarity's activities. It is an instant in which she feels in the hieroglyphic pattern before her a "sense of concealed meaning, of an intent to communicate" (p. 24). This sense of some impending revelation, of words she both wants and fears to hear being spoken out of the void, increases steadily throughout the novel, as she moves amid signs and symbols of communication. The freeways also seem patterned like the printed circuits of a transistor radio; she finds herself living in a motel called Echo Courts; and she learns that the disc jockey to whom she is married thinks of himself, with the aid of LSD, as "an antenna, sending ... [his] pattern out across a million lives" (p. 144). Oedipa finds herself involved with a group of electronics scientists who hold Sinewave Jam Sessions on Saturday nights with "audio oscillators, gunshot machines, contact mikes, everything man" (p. 48); she tries for an ESP message from a profile photograph of Clerk Maxwell on the Nefastis Machine; she seduces one man before a TV set and is propositioned by another who likes to engage in the sexual game while the news from China is on. The largest metaphor of communication, however, is the Tristero system whose possible existence lures Oedipa into scholarly research for the true text of a seventeenth-century play and leads her to wander aimlessly all night through San Francisco, where she witnesses a nether world of secret communication.

As the coincidences blossom, suggesting another "separate, silent, unsuspected world" (p. 125) intruding upon this one, Oedipa becomes "anxious that her revelation not expand beyond a certain point. Lest, possibly, it grow larger than she and assume her to itself." Like Stencil of *V.*, near the end of her inquiry she feels "reluctant about following up anything" (p. 166). Her human contacts with the Tristero disappear or change: her husband takes up LSD; Dr. Hilarius, her shrink, goes mad; Metzger, her co-executor, elopes with a depraved nymphet; her contact at The Greek Way grows mute; but, most important of all, Driblette, the actor-director of the Tristero play, walks into the Pacific, taking his own life.

Deliberately or by accident, Inverarity's will forces Oedipa tentatively to acknowledge that outside of her tower there may not be a void after all, that some "accommodation" may have been "reached, in some kind of dignity, with the Angel of Death." If the Tristero does exist, then there is "another mode of meaning behind the obvious" (p. 182), a meaning aligned, perhaps, with the numinous beauty of truth, with justice, with reason. This is a meaning which others have known and which she could have known "if only she'd looked" (p. 179). If the Tristero does exist, however, the only way one can "continue, and manage to be at all relevant" to the daily world is "as an alien, unfurrowed, assumed full circle into some paranoia." The other side of the proposition is, for her, equally terrifying. If there is no Tristero, she is already "in the orbiting ecstasy of a true paranoia"; the void is real and in it are "only death and the daily, tedious preparations for it" (p. 182).

Although Oedipa is allowed in the last scene of the novel to discover the truth, the reader never learns what this truth is. However, we are given all we need to know: if this world is not the fragmented, disconnected thing it appears to be—dull, out of focus, void of meaning, and leading to death—then its apparent discontinuity is actually held together by a secret, elusive, and transcendent meaning the knowledge of which leads to madness.

[Like Joseph Heller, Thomas Pynchon has] given us novels which show, in Ihab Hassan's phrase, "the deflection of laughter toward anguish."[3] Both have begun with the absurdity of our experience as a premise, and both have forced a vision from their characters at the point of extremity. But here the similarities end, for, in dramatizing the discontinuity which makes up our experience, they have come to highly individualized versions of the reality implied. In what I take to be a non-ominous coincidence, both Yossarian and Stencil flee to Sweden because of what they have seen, the one to fulfill his vision, the other to avoid his fate. Heller, more than Pynchon, realizes the ancient role of comedy in focusing attention upon our betrayals of our own values, while Pynchon probes more relentlessly into the nature of things, and into our modes of knowing, by comic excursions into history.

Pynchon's comedy calls us back not to the sanity and freedom for which Yossarian will save his life or die trying, but to an unblissful but tolerable ignorance in the midst of an absurdity which may be intelligible after all. For all the intellectual activity of his questing characters, Pynchon remains tentative about the value of the intellect. In the pursuance of his quest, Stencil acquires a fulfilling sense of animateness. But with the prospect of ending the quest, of making the connections, comes an apocalyptic vision of an absolute threat to life. The threat is not simply from death which, metaphorically, would be right enough, but from the take-over of the inanimate that promises to reduce the whole human enterprise to something utterly meaningless. While "the unnamable act, the recognition, the Word" (p. 180) of which Oedipa awaits sure knowledge at the end of her quest does not threaten absolutely, it does require, at least, an even more disjunctive, paranoid condition than has already characterized her experience. Thus Pynchon's two novels end in a peculiar kind of misologism, for the perception of rational connections in experience is rejected not because it does not tell us the truth, but because it does.

NOTES

2. Thomas Pynchon, *The Crying of Lot 49* (Philadelphia: J. B. Lippincott Co., 1966), p. 124. Subsequent references to this novel appear in parentheses following the quotation.

3. "Laughter in the Dark: The New Voice in American Fiction," *American Scholar*, 33 (Autumn, 1964): 637.

—John Hunt, "Comic Escape and Anti-Vision: *V.* and *The Crying of Lot 49*." *Critical Essays on Thomas Pynchon*, edited by Richard Pearce, (Boston: G.K. Hall & Co., 1981): 32, 38–41.

TONY TANNER ON THE FUNCTION OF ENTROPY

[Tony Tanner was Professor of English at Cambridge University. His publications include *The American Mystery: American Literature from Emerson to DeLillo*, *The Reign of Wonder*, *City of Words*, and *Adultery in the Novel*. Here, Tanner suggests that the conflict between the entropy of information and the entropy of thermodynamics drives the novel and gives it its meaning.]

The Crying of Lot 49 (1966) is one of the most deceptive—as well as one of the most brilliant—short novels to have appeared since the last war. It is a strange book in that the more we learn the more mysterious everything becomes. The more we *think* we know, the less we *know* we know. The model for the story would seem to be the Californian detective story—an established tradition including the works of writers such is Raymond Chandler, Ross MacDonald and Eric Stanley Gardner. But in fact it works in a reverse direction. With a detective story you start with a mystery and move towards a final clarification, all the apparently disparate, suggestive bits of evidence finally being bound together in one illuminating pattern; whereas in Pynchon's novel we move from a state of degree-zero mystery—just the quotidian mixture of an average Californian day—to a condition of increasing mystery and dubiety.

In the simplest terms, the novel concerns Oedipa Maas, who learns that she has been named as an executor ('or she supposed executrix', p. 1) of the estate of a deceased Californian real-estate mogul named Pierce Inverarity. As she sets about exploring this 'estate', she seems to discover more and more clues indicating the existence of an underground, anarchic organization called the Tristero, which, possibly dating from thirteenth-century Europe, seems to oppose all the official lines of communication and have its own secret system of communication. Seems. She can never be sure whether she is discovering a real organization, or is the victim of a gigantic hoax, or is wildly hallucinating. Her search or quest clearly has wider implications, for we are told that Pierce Inverarity was 'a founding father' (p. 14), and near the end we read: 'She had dedicated herself, weeks ago, to making sense of what Inverarity had left behind, never suspecting that the legacy was America' (p. 134).

So on one level the driving question is simply: what does a contemporary American 'inherit' from the country's past? On the title-page Pynchon included this note: 'A portion of this novel was first published in *Esquire* magazine under the title "The World (This one), the Flesh (Mrs Oedipa Maas), and the Testament of Pierce Inverarity".' Since he did not choose to give the title of another extract that appeared in a magazine, we may infer that he wanted this title definitely to appear under the main title of the book. Of course it raises the question: is 'the

Testament of Pierce Inverarity' the Devil (following the World and the Flesh)? Like so much in the book it remains a question. The name itself can suggest either un-truth or in-the-truth; I have seen it glossed is 'pierces or peers into variety' and 'inverse' and 'rarity'. But then names can be like that in Pynchon's work, and I shall return to this point in a moment. The last phone call Oedipa receives from Pierce Inverarity is literally multivocal: he speaks in 'heavy Slavic tones', 'comic-Negro', 'hostile Pachuco dialect', as 'a Gestapo officer', and finally 'his Lamont Cranston voice'. He does indeed speak in many 'tongues'; the problem is which, if any of them, is 'true'? The phone call itself comes from 'where she would never know', and the 'phone line could have pointed any direction, any length' (pp. 2–3). Origin, intention, extension—all are insolubly ambiguous. What is Oedipa Maas hearing? What should she listen to? Is it all cacophony? Or is she being somehow singled out for 'revelations'? (...)

While the word 'Tristero' preoccupies Oedipa, another word equally bothers another of the 'leads' she meets, John Nefastis, and that word—so important in Pynchon—is 'entropy'. As Nefastis explains, 'there were two distinct kinds of this entropy. One having to do with heat-engines, the other to do with communication' (p. 77). Nefastis has a 'machine' based on the Scotch scientist Clerk Maxwell's postulation of something known as Maxwell's Demon. This machine (which Nefastis his tried to make literal) suggests a situation in which there is a box of molecules moving at different speeds and in which 'the Demon' could simply sort out the slow ones from the fast ones: this would create a region of high temperature which could be used to drive a heat engine. 'Since the Demon only sat and sorted, you wouldn't have put any real work into the system. So you would be violating the Second Law of Thermodynamics, getting something for nothing, causing perpetual motion!' To which Oedipa sceptically replies: 'Sorting isn't work?'

The problem here centres on the fact that there seems to be an opposition between thermodynamic entropy and entropy in information theory. As thermodynamic entropy increases in a system, variety and potential diminish, and the certainty of information about the system increases. However, in information theory, 'entropy' refers to the measure of uncertainty in a system. Put very crudely, we can say this: in a thermodynamic system, as things tend towards stagnation, repetition, predictability, they approach a terminal state in which there is no more energy available for new work; in information theory, the higher the degree of disorganization, noise, uncertainty, the more possibility there is for new signals, new information. Nefastis tries to explain:

> She did gather that there were two distinct kinds of this entropy. One having to do with heat engines, the other to do with communication. The equation for one, back in the 30's, had looked very like the equation for the other. It was a coincidence. The two fields were entirely unconnected, except at one point: Maxwell's Demon. As the Demon sat and sorted his molecules into hot and cold, the system was said to lose entropy. But somehow the loss was offset by the information the Demon gained about what molecules were where.
> 'Communication is the key,' cried Nefastis.... 'Entropy is a figure of speech, then, a Metaphor. It connects the world of thermodynamics to the world of information flow. The Machine uses both. The Demon makes the metaphor not only verbally graceful, but also objectively true.' (p. 77) (...)

The problem is finally about America. There is the America of San Narciso, but is there perhaps another America? An America of the 'disinherited' (but 'What was left to inherit?' Oedipa wonders (p. 135))—transients, squatters, drifters, exiles within the system, people existing in the invisible interstices of official society, like those who live 'among a web of telephone wires, living in the very copper rigging and secular miracle of communication, untroubled by the dumb voltages flickering their miles, the night long, in the thousands of unheard messages' (p. 135). The Tristero system might be a great hoax; but it might be 'all true' (p. 134). And here is perhaps the most crucial and one of the most eloquent and powerful passages in the book:

Who knew? Perhaps she'd be hounded someday as far as joining Tristero itself, if it existed, in its twilight, its aloofness, its waiting. The waiting above all; if not for another set of possibilities to replace those that had conditioned the land to accept any San Narciso among its most tender flesh without a reflex or a cry, then at least, at the very least, waiting for a symmetry of choices to break down, to go skew. She had heard all about excluded middles; they were bad shit, to be avoided; and how had it ever happened here, with the chances once so good for diversity? For it was now like walking among matrices of a great digital computer, the zeroes and ones twinned above, hanging like balanced mobiles right and left, ahead, thick, maybe endless. Behind the hieroglyphic streets there would be either a transcendent meaning, or only the earth.... Ones and zeroes, So did the couples arrange themselves.... Another mode of meaning behind the obvious, or none. Either Oedipa in the orbiting ecstasy of a true paranoia, or a real Tristero. For there either was some Tristero beyond the appearance of the legacy America, or there was just America and if there was just America then it seemed the only way she could continue, and manage to be at all relevant to it, was as an alien, unfurrowed, assumed full circle into some paranoia. (pp. 136–7)

The law of the 'excluded middle'—as I understand it—is that a statement is either true or false. There cannot be anything in between. Either it is raining, or it is not. Yet there are those strange, atmospheric conditions, not easily classifiable, in which moistness and dryness seem strangely mixed, which might make us—illogically, unphilosophically—long to admit the 'excluded middle', a middle term for something real but unascertainable. Oedipa is not at ease in a world of binary oppositions—ones and zeroes. Recall that apparently incomprehensible sentence in which it was stated that she would have revelations 'about what remained yet had somehow, before this, stayed away'. The law of the excluded middle would say that either it was there or it was not there. Quite apart from considerations of logic, such a rigidity forecloses on the possibility of unforeseen 'diversity' and irresolvable dubiety. Yet it is into just such an area of possible diversity and dubiety that Oedipa has stumbled—and we, as readers, along with her. Oedipa is mentally in a world of 'if' and 'perhaps', walking through an accredited world of either/or. It is part of her pain, her dilemma and, perhaps, her emancipation. At the auction which concludes the book, leaving all in suspension, the auctioneer is indeed likened to a priest—but also to a 'puppet-master'. There is no way in which Oedipa can be sure just what kind of 'performance' she has been—is—present at. And there is no way in which we can, either. And yet, at the end, as we both finish and wait to begin, something—and this is part of the deceptive magic of the book—seems to remain. Even while it stays away.

—Tony Tanner. "*The Crying of Lot 49.*" *Thomas Pynchon*, (London: Methuen, 1982): 56–57, 66–67, 71–73.

PLOT SUMMARY OF
V.

Described as "wild," "macabre," "picaresque," and above all a staggering work of genius, *V.*, the first of Pynchon's novels to be published and which almost immediately brought him national and international acclaim, was published in 1963. To summarize *V.* as the story of a man's search for the mysterious and perhaps dangerous woman named V. is correct, but as the novel in its entirety describes, "correctness" and truth are two wildly different things. While the novel is either difficult or impossible to summarize, there are two main threads or plots to its structure, threads that begin far apart from each other but ultimately intersect and interweave, forming a "V" in the plot itself. One storyline of the book details the life and adventures of Benny Profane and is set in the mid 1950s; the other line of the book describes Herbert Stencil's quest for V. "herself," and includes most of the key, calamitous events of the twentieth century.

The novel begins on Christmas Eve, 1955, in Norfolk, Virginia, where the streetlights recede in an asymmetric V. Right away, we are introduced to Benny Profane—a former sailor but more to the point, "a schlemihl and human yo-yo." Profane travels to The Sailor's Grave, a rowdy bar in which sailors and Marines are having a brawl, and we are presently cast among a host of colorful if not absurd characters from Benny's past: Pig Bodine, Mrs. Buffo, Pappy Hod, Beatrice, Ploy, Dewey Gland, and Paola Maijstral, a mysterious barmaid from Malta.

The first two chapters of the book then chart both Benny's current activities and the events of his recent past, including his yo-yo-like travels as a roadworker up and down the east coast and his relationship with the lovely and quirky Rachel Owlglass, who loves—literally—her MG. Ultimately, Benny and Paola travel to New York, where they share adventures of sorts with "The Whole Sick Crew," a group of even odder characters than the denizens of The Sailor's Grave. For work, Benny volunteers for the alligator hunting patrol in the sewers beneath the city.

After these "profane" chapters, the book turns to the "sacred" quest of Herbert Stencil, a "quick change artist" who refers to himself in the third person, and the son of a man from the British Foreign Office who died in 1919 when a waterspout sunk the ship on which he was sailing. Since 1945, the younger Stencil has been fighting to find out the true identity of V., a woman referred to in his father's journal. At the tail end of the nineteenth century the elder Stencil had written, "There is more behind and inside V. than any of us had suspected. Not who, but what: what is she," and based on this, Herbert suspects that V. has been part of a "grand conspiracy" leading up to and indeed bringing about not only the first but also the second World War. We see a "disguised" Stencil in the background of eight different vignettes as several characters observe an unfolding plot possibly related to V. herself: Aieul the waiter and "amateur libertine," Yusef the factotum, the penniless rogue Maxwell Rowley-Bugge, Waldetar the conductor, a poor Arab cabdriver named Gebrail, Girgis the burglar, Hanne, a barmaid, and the theatre where a murder takes place.

From this point on, the book itself becomes a kind of yo-yo, alternating between raucous scenes of Profane and "The Whole Sick Crew," and scenes of the obsessive Stencil tracking his target. Although at times, just as the yo-yo's up and down motions become one another at the top and bottom of its trajectory, Profane and Stencil appear together, most often they inhabit separate, though connected and intermeshed realities, Stencil seeking for the truth behind certainty and Profane accepting what comes his way.

Again, while any true summary might be impossible to create, there are several passages in the novel that stand out and which help both to clarify the overall themes of the novel and to make the job of working though it easier.

Chapter 4 contains a famous scene in which Esther's nose job is described in violent and graphic terms. Shale Schoenmaker, Esther's plastic surgeon, coerces Esther to have sex with him and she becomes pregnant. We also hear about Schoenmaker's past and are introduced to the World War I pilot, Evan Godolphin. As a young grease monkey repairing planes, Schoenmaker worshipped the pilot. Godolphin's face was disfigured in a plane crash, but his features were partially restored through plastic surgery, at which point Schoenmaker decided to devote himself to plastic surgery as well.

In Chapter 5, "In which Stencil nearly goes West with an alligator," Benny chases an alligator through the New York sewers. Underground, Profane stumbles across "Fairing's Parish," named for a depression-era priest who descended to the sewers to convert the rats, whom he believed would one day rule the city. Finally cornering the alligator, Profane takes his first kill, though he finds that his heart is not really in it. Do the alligators, he wonders, welcome their deaths? Benny also fires at what he thinks is another alligator, but later it is revealed that it was Stencil, prowling through the sewers in wetsuit, mask, and snorkel.

As we learn in Chapter 6, "In which Profane returns to street level," Benny has always believed that the inanimate world is out to get him, and that world includes women as one of its objects. This theme, which mirrors the entropic nature of a universe in which life is constantly on the verge of being eradicated, is evident in the way that women have always "happened" to Profane, as if by accident. As a case in point, Fina, one of his coworker's sisters, "happens" to him. She is the "spiritual leader" or "den mother" of a gang called the Playboys, but as Profane knows, that simply means that at some point she will be gang raped by them. Unable to stop the course of events as it unfolds, and unable to defend Fina when her brother beats her for being raped, Benny decides to retire from the Alligator Patrol.

In Chapter 7, "She hangs on the western wall," dentist Dudley Eigenvalue shows Stencil the false teeth he has constructed, though for whom they are intended is impossible to answer—just as the question "Who then is V.?" is impossible to answer for Stencil. For as he says, "Psychodontia has it secrets and so does Stencil ... but most important, so does V. She's yielded him only the poor skeleton of a dossier. Most of what he has is inference. He doesn't know who she is, nor what she is. He's trying to find out. As a legacy from his father."

Chapter 9, "Mondaugen's story," is one of the key passages in the book, both in terms of the theme of undecideability in the book and its concern with history and the atrocities of the twentieth century. As told to Stencil by Mondaugen himself, Mondaugen was assigned to the Sudwest Protectorate in 1922 to record atmospheric radio disturbances called sferics, but his observations are interrupted by The Great Herero Uprising. Mondaugen later works at Peenemunde on German rockets, and finally comes to America to work for Yoyodyne—the same corporation we first encountered in *The Crying of Lot 49*.

Mondaugen explains that as he was looking at the jury-rigged oscillograph recording of the sferics he began to see traces of something in the fluctuations—a kind of code, he says—but one which could never be broken, just as the book itself is a kind of code for its readers: we know that the words on the page are not really full of specific *meaning*, but rather serve only as links between what we would like to think is there and what we suspect is "really" there. Thus, against the "certain" historical slaughter of the Herero, Pynchon juxtaposes the "uncertain" meaning of meaning itself in order to present a much more mechanistic, much more appalling background to the way so-called reality works: "We are, perhaps, the lead weights of a fantastic clock, necessary to keep it in motion, to keep an ordered sense of history and time prevailing against chaos." Not doing any meaningful work, merely doing; not the causes but the effects, the symptoms; fighting thermodynamics in local systems, mere eddies in much more powerful currents, creating and sustaining illusions, quests, and obsessions merely to protect ourselves from entropy and chaos.

In Chapter 11, "Confessions of Fausto Maijstral," which takes place in Malta, Fausto discusses both the birth of his daughter Paola, and the bombing of Malta during the war. Most importantly, Fausto details information on another of V.'s guises/appearances: Fausto observed the partially inanimate "Bad Priest" and/or Victoria Wren being disassembled by a group of children.

In Chapter 13, "In which the yo-yo string is revealed as a state of mind," Stencil spells out the nature of his quest to Benny and asks Profane to travel with him to Malta. During a walk with

Stencil, Benny realizes he is close to his parent's home and stops in to see them. Finding no one at home but a meal laid out for him as if by accident, Benny dines, leaving traces of his eaten food as a sign he was there.

Another key passage occurs in Chapter 14, "V. In Love." While seemingly identifying V. herself through the title and through a direct line in the text—"If we've not already guessed, 'the woman' is, again, the lady V."—this "certainty" is ultimately no closer to the "truth" about V. than any other of the myriad possibilities—though by now we perhaps have more of a quantum sense of V. and must use the term *probabilities*—for V.'s identity.

As the novel begins to wind down and/or up in the final chapter, all the loose threads seem to come together but are just as soon found to be even more disconnected than before. Stencil who had thought he'd solved the mystery, realizes that here is and probably always will be more clues to discover, and the last we hear of him is in a note left on Benny while he sleeps off a tremendous hangover: the note tells us that Stencil is off to Stockholm to continue the holy quest, perhaps forever. As for Benny, alone and being supported temporarily by Maijstral, he meets an American college girl and poet named Brenda Wigglesworth who tells him, "I am the twentieth century." Finding an inexplicable attraction for and understanding of each other, the last we see of Profane is him running hand-in-hand with Brenda through the ruins of Valleta, running in a mood and mode reminiscent of Kerouac, running "through the abruptly absolute night, momentum alone carrying them toward the edge of Malta, and the Mediterranean beyond."

After the last chapter, there remains the enigmatic Epilogue, which presents the last days and seconds of Stencil's father, Sidney. In the Epilogue, nearly all of the characters who have prompted, aided, and hindered Stencil's quest come together: Veronica Manganese, Maijstral, Godolphin, Father Fairing, and others. Apparently answering many of the novel's multitude of questions—for one thing, it seems almost certain that V. is in fact the elder Stencil's lover and quite probably the Younger's mother—at the very end of the novel all of our certainty, and

51

perhaps even our eternal attachment to the concept of "certainty" are wracked: the ship on which the elder Stencil is sailing encounters—out of nowhere and with no warning—a waterspout, which lifts it high into the air then slams it down into the sea, killing all aboard.

While it's possible to suggest that *V.* is a maze *not* without form or meaning, the real maze that *V.* creates, or invokes, or evokes, is the maze of certainty or meaning that readers often attempt to splice into life and literature, both. Time and again the narration of the book forces us to encounter the meaninglessness and uncertainty of the book, and ultimately it poses a question: what made us even think of "certainty" in the first place?

Finally, what makes the book great, beyond its erudition, panache, and energy, is that Pynchon doesn't simply expect readers to accept his ideas, but rather he demonstrates them as he presents them: instead of simply suggesting the probabilities outside of meaning for writing, he creates a book without meaning or form and makes it work. The idea that V. may not be anything at all, that "she" may be at most a pattern or an obsession that skirts reality and exchange, defies commodity, and doesn't seem to matter to Stencil. His quest or obsession doesn't have to *mean* anything, as long as it *is*. Just "trying to find out" is not only enough, it is all Stencil or we can really hope for.

LIST OF CHARACTERS IN
V.

Benny Profane is one of the two main characters in the novel. A Catholic-Jew and former sailor, Benny was born during the Depression and at the start of the novel is in the middle of his career as a human yo-yo and overall schlemihl—that is, a victim's victim, a silent, passive man beset by the inanimate. Never sure of what he wants or even what he is exactly, and more interested in the past than the present or the future, he seems most like a particle buffeted by forces he neither understands nor anticipates. In terms of love, Benny is lucky with neither Paola, Rachel, nor Fina, but at the end of the novel he seems to have met his equal in Brenda—but at the same time, at the novel's conclusion Benny disappears, literally, into the night.

Herbert Stencil, the other main character of the novel, was born at the beginning of the century. A man of action as opposed to the ultra-passive Profane, he is the son of Sidney Stencil and an unknown woman who either died in childbirth or who ran off soon after. Obsessed with discovering both the truth behind V. and the secret history of the twentieth century, Stencil is both a quick-change artist and a teller of tales. What exactly motivates him is unclear—boredom, desire, the need for pure action, a desire for his own death?—but in a way strangely like his "opposite," Benny, Stencil seems as much driven by accident as anything else.

Herbert's father, **Sidney Stencil**, served in the Foreign Office until his death in 1919. The journal he leaves behind and his cryptic entry about V. sets Herbert on the obsessive course that will rule and/or ruin his entire life.

Not, strictly speaking, a character, possibly not even a single person, and perhaps not a person at all, **V.** nevertheless dominates the entire novel. Existing possibly only because Stencil is tracking her down, she-they-it appears in numerous guises throughout the book and across the twentieth century: at one point or another in the novel V. may be a painting, a pure concept, a sewer rat, a force of history, a sailing ship, a woman or women named Victoria, Vera, and/or Veronica, a Parisian dress shop owner, a machine, the Bad Priest, the host of V-shapes that haunt the novel, or any number of any possibilities, including the twentieth century itself. Specifically, but hard to nail down, too, V. may in fact be Stencil's mother.

Also not a single character but a motley of "disaffected" characters, **The Whole Sick Crew** functions almost as a single person and can best be described as a frolicsome group of hooligans, a "beat" collection of misfits who stand in contrast to and at the same time help to define and delineate America in the fifties. As a rule they are "all talk" and are more interested in process and experience than stasis and simply being. Though encompassing many different people, the Crew's most common members include Profane, Rachel, Pig Bodine, Esther, Melvin, Fergus, Raoul, Slab, Charisma, Fu, Mafia, and Winsome.

Two members of the Crew, **Rachel** and **Pig**, warrant individual mention:
Rachel Owlglass is from the "Five Towns" area of Long Island and comes in and out of Benny's life: in fact, she meets him for the "first time" twice. At times it seems as if she is love with Benny, at others she seems wholly uninterested in him and his life. An impetuous and eccentric woman, Rachel is also somewhat kinky: at one point in the book, Benny watches her as she makes love to her MG.

Pig Bodine is a former shipmate of Benny's from the USS Scaffold and member of the Whole Sick Crew who spends much of the novel either drunk, sexually aggressive, fighting, in jail, or AWOL. A shameless eavesdropper and Peeping Tom, Bodine believes that "life is the most precious possession you have," but he also tries to rape Paola. An interesting character across Pynchon's work, he appears again *Gravity's Rainbow*, while one of his ancestors makes an appearance in *Mason & Dixon*.

The Godolphins: Evan and his father **Hugh**. Hugh was an officer in the British Navy who also made a fruitless expedition to the South Pole to discover Vheissu. Hugh becomes acquainted with Victoria Wren—one of the possible guises of V.—and appears in Africa during the Herero Uprising. His son Evan was a World War I aviator whose face was horribly disfigured and who appears in the novel as part of as ongoing conspiracy that may have led to the start of the second World War. Having met Victoria Wren, he later becomes the caretaker of Veronica Manganese's (who may also be Victoria and/or V. herself) mansion.

The Maijstrals: Fausto Senior, Carla, Paola and **Fausto Junior**. Old Fausto works in the shipyards on Malta and as a spy for the British Foreign Office. He is married to Carla, who is much younger than he and who is given to suicidal thoughts. Young Fausto, who is Paola's father, may have made it into the world because of the good graces of the Older Stencil which in his mind makes him Herbert's "brother." Paola Maijstral, barmaid at the Sailor's Grave and on-again-off-again wife of Pappy Hod, is in some ways passive and victimized as Benny is, and in other ways is a woman of action and decisiveness, as Herbert is.

The Mendozas: Angel and **Josefina**. Josefina, or Fina, is at one time the object of Benny's affection, but is more important in the novel because of her role as "Den Mother" of the Playboys, a New York street gang who later gang rape her. Angel, Fina's brother, is one of Benny's coworkers in the Alligator Patrol who, upon learning of Fina's rape, beats her after being unable to protect her.

Kurt Mondaugen, who also figures prominently in *Gravity's Rainbow*, is a young German engineer who witnesses the Herero Uprising while studying sferics in Africa.

Mr. Goodfellow, a "fat Englishman," is an agent of the British Foreign Office and lover of Victoria Wren.

Dudley Eigenvalue is a New York dentist who has built a set of metal dentures—perhaps for, perhaps from V.

Esther Harvitz is Rachel and Paola's roommate. After getting a nose job from Schoenmaker, she has sex with him and becomes pregnant.

Shale Schoenmaker, who may own "a vital piece of the V. jigsaw," is a plastic surgeon who devoted his life to the field when his idol, Evan Godolphin's disfigured face was partially rebuilt. He performs a graphic nose job on Esther and later forces her to have sex with him.

CRITICAL VIEWS ON
V.

KENNETH KUPSCH ON THE TRUE IDENTITY OF V.

[Kenneth Kupsch is a graduate of Rutgers University and is currently working on a collection of short stories. Here Kupsch suggests that far from being mysterious, diffuse, or otherwise unknowable, the identity and nature of V. are openly given in the novel.]

Thomas Pynchon's novel *V.* has been described as everything from "the most masterful first novel in the history of literature" (Poirier 167) to "a riddle that, once correctly answered, never taxes the mind again" (Sklar 90). While it may very well stand as the former, it most assuredly cannot be construed as the latter, if only because the proposition has never actually been tested. Up to now, Pynchon supporters and detractors alike have tended to evade the question "Who or what is V.?" and have assumed it to be either purposely insoluble or simply irrelevant. To the extent that anyone has seriously bothered to tackle the question in recent years, the answer usually resembles that put forward by Edward Mendelson, who sees in it only an elaboration of the simple idea of "the decline of the animate into the inanimate" (6). To this one might well ask: but what of all those inanimate things in the book that have become animate? It is my contention that there is a knowable, unequivocal, and essentially irrefutable answer to the question, and that far from releasing the reader from any further obligation to the work, knowing that answer heightens one's obligation to it.

Here we may begin to see the way in which Pynchon set out in *V.* not simply to parody forms he was in the end imitating, but rather to challenge basic assumptions and formulae of detective and historical fictions, while at the same time adhering to their most traditional demands. For example, the matter of resolution: since the author has asked the question "Who is V.?," is it not reasonable to expect, to demand even, that he answer it?

Certainly most readers of detective fiction would think so. The weakness of much of the genre derives not so much from its unreasonable demands as from its often cheap solutions, wherein solving the riddle (as Robert Sklar suggests) becomes the only intelligible point to the exercise. At the same time, it strikes me that far too many critics—admirers and detractors both—have assumed rather easily that either Pynchon was not obliged to solve his own riddle or he simply wasn't up to the task. Neither point of view is correct. For not only did Pynchon satisfy the basic demand of the form (that is, answer the novel's central question) but, more remarkably, he did so in a way that instead of closing the book, opens it up to nearly infinite reflection on its vast, magnificent, and unmistakable architectural design. Stated more specifically, it is by knowing who V. is, and more specifically still, who V. has become by the "present" of the book, that the reader will be able to make sense of why things are the way they are at that time. Looked at another way, one-half of the novel (the historical episodes) is devoted to solving the riddle of V., while the other half (the contemporary episodes) is devoted to making use of that solution.

That the question of V.'s identity is answerable, and what is more, that Stencil answers it, is very easily demonstrated. In the contemporary episode that precedes the epilogue, Stencil interviews Father Avalanche. The previous night, after speaking to Fausto Maijstral, Stencil had become nearly convinced that "it did add up only to the recurrence of an initial and a few dead objects" (445). But after learning that Avalanche's predecessor on Malta had been Father Fairing, Stencil mutters to himself unequivocally: "Clinches it" (449). Later he adds: "Stencil came on Father Fairing's name once, apparently by accident. Today he came on it again, by what only could have been design" (450). Two days later Stencil is gone to Stockholm to chase what he describes as "the frayed end of another clue" (452). More importantly, he is gone as a character from the book, and we are left with an epilogue whose very title confirms that indeed the story has already reached its end. Yet, simply stated, if the question of V. were not itself also by implication resolved, then the story of *V.* could not in any truly artistically defensible sense lay claim to having reached its ultimate conclusion. Stencil's behavior here is thus a very important clue: he has proved the answer, though by no means exhausted it, any more than proving the Copernican theory exhausted the field of astronomy. On the contrary, and as we shall see, Stencil continues his quest at the novel's end, not because he is some quaintly obsessed madman who simply refuses to accept the idea of the unanswerable, but rather because knowing that answer has given his quest all the more meaning and importance, and has given all future evidence its proper place in the overall architectural scheme.

However, before one can hope to find the correct solution to the question of V., it will be helpful to observe some of the reasons why its discovery has been so elusive. As I have stated, Pynchon set out not merely to challenge the familiar conventions of plot, characterization, resolution, and so on in detective and historical fiction, but to do so in the most artistic manner possible. That is, he chose to seek original means of presentation and resolution to well-established but largely static literary traditions. And nowhere is this more true in *V.* than in the very nature of the object of its quest. Most fictions organized around the idea of a quest—detective stories being among them—tend to resolve in one of three ways: the thing sought turns out to be (1) an object of some kind, such as the Holy Grail, Charles Foster Kane's sled, or a large sum of money; (2) a person (the clever murderer in the standard detective novel); or (3) a cabal of shadowy and manipulative people or institutions. (This last category, comprising what have come to be known as conspiracy tales and including everything from *Rosemary's Baby* to Pynchon's own *Gravity's Rainbow*, has surely been one of the most fecund developments in modern fiction.) But in *V.*, Pynchon's first and still most original work of major fiction, he chose something new, and he chose to reveal it in a most original and demanding way.

Certainly at the time Pynchon was writing *V.*, no formula in the detective genre had gone more adamantly unchallenged than the manner in which evidence was revealed to its readers. All evidence would lead to, and ultimately be validated or invalidated by, a so-called smoking gun. Indeed, no single phrase or idea has more clearly come out of the tradition of the detective story and taken its place in everyday speech than that of the smoking gun. But how often in life does smoking-gun evidence actually appear to prove a thing is so? Or for that matter, how often does the lack of such evidence, depending on the quality and quantity of other existing evidence, dissuade intelligent observers of a thing's unqualified veracity? At what point, for instance, in the history of astronomy (Copernicus? Tycho Brahe? Kepler? Galileo? Newton?) did proof of the heliocentric view of the solar system become little more than a formal rubber stamp of what was already understood to be true? It was, in fact, considerably after Newton's time that telescopes were developed accurate enough to measure the minute changes in the positions of nearby stars, a desideratum to proving that the earth moved around the sun. Yet by the time that proof came, no educated person, let alone scientist, imagined it would be otherwise. When, in other words, did the circumstantial evidence so overwhelm as to become essentially irrefutable? Such is usually the way in science. Is it surprising, then, to think that a writer whose scientific background has so often been observed and commented on should have adhered to and found literary inspiration in an aspect of that background so basic to it? Nevertheless, readers have apparently been so bound by the convention of the detective form that they remain willing to assume that the lack of smoking-gun evidence means that no certain answer can really exist. The only thing missing from the solution to *V.*'s central mystery is the smoking gun. However, despite this lack, Stencil *knows* he has solved the mystery of V., and Pynchon seals the fact by ending the story proper and adding an epilogue. Thus it is important to recognize what kind of evidence Pynchon intends his readers to seek, and on what basis they can, like Stencil, hope to solve the mystery. (...)

Benny's indistinct and uncompelling nature as a character raises an important question: if passive Benny is more character type than character, why does he play so prominent a role in the novel? Having already discussed a number of the ways in which Pynchon devised *V.* to avoid some of the worst clichés of detective and other forms of quest fiction, I should note how many of those ways depend on the idea of V. as the specific chain of motive forces that this essay has demonstrated her to be. Yet there is one other notable convention of the genre that Pynchon manages to sidestep, one that helps explain Benny's significant place in the work—the cliché of the red herring.

It would, of course, be inept to abandon even the most overworked cliché without substituting something that could function quite as well. (Many pretentious works presume to parody their superiors, but really only succeed in demonstrating why a cliché has become a cliché.) In order to see how *V.* manages without the red herring that flourishes in so much detective fiction, it will be helpful to first look at an example of what might be confused with a traditional use of the device. Consider the story of Vheissu. Since it is now clear that Vheissu is *not* the answer to the question "Who or what is V.?" then this story would seem to have functioned to distract the reader's attention from any premature discovery of the answer to the book's central mystery. And in a sense it has. But here again, let us view the thing a little more closely and carefully. By what artistic right should the story of Vheissu have merited inclusion in a work entitled *V.*? I have already established that *V.* is not an all-inclusive phenomenon. Rather, it is like the articles in a single volume of an encyclopedia: numerous, wide-ranging, and connected by the fact that each entry begins with the common letter. However, in the case of Pynchon's novel, that letter is not the connecting point. Instead, what connects everything is the *history of V.* To whom, after all, does old Godolphin tell his story, with its almost mythical overtones (most obviously reminiscent of the latter sections of Poe's *The Narrative of Arthur Gordon Pym*)? Simply stated, he tells it to V., thus connecting it to her and making it a part of the biography of her existence. In this sense, it is no red herring at all. Moreover, its coincident themes not only shed greater light on the book's larger ones, but actually help to create them. What serves as the longest running "red herring" turns out to be the story of Father Fairing, which is introduced in chapter 5, but whose connection to V. is not revealed until the penultimate chapter. Appropriately, it is this final connection that effectively pushes Stencil's theory over the top and justifies his claim: "Clinches it."

Which brings us back to Benny. It is important to realize that Benny is not a victim of V.'s powers per se; he is, it must be admitted, a technological "schlemihl" (among other kinds), out of tune with the thinking and movement of the modern world. His inability to adapt to the increasingly mechanized world around him is simply the most recent and obvious development pushing him around and making him into a victim; his passive nature and character type is really much older than V.—it is as old as the human race itself. What thematically justifies his elevated status in the novel is not so much what has happened to him as what has begun to happen to so many others around him, and which can be most clearly seen by comparison to him: as a result of V.'s most recent emanation as a motive force, more and more characters have come in one way or another to resemble him in his inanimateness. And to this extent, at least, Pynchon may be said to have successfully dramatized his themes through characterization. As for what can be said to more directly justify Benny's appearance in the novel, by now it should be obvious: his direct connection to V. through Stencil. Of course, this presumes that Stencil is the son of V., and as such her unwitting agent, but that is a fact the novel never challenges. Draw a straight line between two points. Call one point a mystery and the other the solution. This is the astonishing first novel Thomas Pynchon created, and which has kept many of the most skillful and experienced readers guessing for over 30 years.

—Kenneth Kupsch, "Finding V." *Twentieth Century Literature: A Scholarly and Critical Journal* 44, no. 4 (1998): 428–31, 444–45.

MARK SANDERS ON THE CRITIQUE OF TRADITIONAL HISTORY

[Mark Sanders is Assistant Professor of English and American Literature at Brandeis University. He has published essays in *Research in African Literatures, Critique: Studies in Contemporary Fiction, Law Text Culture,* and *the Journal of Southern African Studies*. In this essay he asserts that part of Pynchon's project in the novel is to create a valid alternative exploration of historical events.]

A letter written in January 1969 was the occasion for Thomas Pynchon to define his fictional project in *V.* and *Gravity's Rainbow* in historiographical terms and to state some ground rules for the metropolitan historian of European colonialism in Africa. In seeking to explain colonialism, that historian has to make sure of "getting the African side of it" (Seed 241). The historian also is dogged not only by the biases of official colonial historiography and by European writers who interpret African belief systems in Western Christian terms but by the nature and processes of writing itself. Pynchon the novelist assumes that what unites him with the historian of colonialism is his desire for historical explanation, but he differentiates himself from the latter by claiming a certain archival ineptitude.

He dramatizes that difference when he reviews his reading for *Gravity's Rainbow* and registers a preference for ethnographical studies over reports of the South African government that he consulted in the course of his more random research for *V.* "I'm afraid I went at the whole thing in a kind of haphazard fashion," Pynchon wrote Thomas F. Hirsch, a graduate history student interested in the Bondelzwarts uprising, an intriguing yet underdocumented and, at the time, little-researched episode in the history of Namibia, a country known as South-West Africa for the first eighty-nine years of this century. "[I] was actually looking for a report on Malta and happened to find the Bondelzwarts one right next to it in the same, what the NY Public Library calls, 'pamphlet volume.' But since then I've been hooked on it.... For some reason I can't leave [the Südwest material] alone" (Seed 240, cf. Cowart 139n). In the course of half-a-dozen years, Pynchon has moved on from that chance encounter with the Bondelzwarts to a study of the customs of the Hereros, whose decimation in the aftermath of a three-year war against the German Army is sketched in *V.*: "I was thinking of the 1904 campaign" (Seed 240). Saying he was unable, he says, to offer Hirsch much bibliographical assistance, Pynchon meditates at length to "clarify" his current project, all the while misplacing the memory of a crucial document. He recalls in time, in a postscript to the letter, "a British propaganda pamphlet printed around 1917" (Seed 243). *The Report on the Natives of South-West Africa and their Treatment by Germany* (1918), which publicized the Herero genocide, is the principal source for "Mondaugen's story."

    The letter to Hirsch not only sheds light on the processes of *V.*'s composition, but on what Pynchon regarded as the limits of what he could do with his sources. The ethnographical material, although more respectable than the propaganda, has its own difficulties. Pynchon tells Hirsch: "The problem as I guess you appreciate, with getting the African side of it, is that the Hereros were preliterate and everything available from them is (a) anecdotal and (b) filtered through the literate (McLuhan), Western, Christian biases of European reporters, usually missionaries" (Seed 241). The Namibian Hereros become, for Pynchon, representative Africans, and in turn, stand for others who have been brought into contact with Western colonialism and imperialism, a process he often characterizes as psychocultural subjection. Herero becomes a universal name. The events in South-West Africa are, "I don't like to use the word ... archtypical [sic] of every clash between the west and non-west, clashes that are still going on right now in South East Asia" (Seed 242). Events in Vietnam follow the same patterns as previous colonial situations, "the imposition of a culture valuing analysis and differentiation on a culture that valued unity and integration" (Seed 241). The ethnographical literature will go some way toward helping Pynchon to redress, in the process of writing *Gravity's Rainbow*, the biases inherent in European accounts of the Hereros. Nevertheless, Pynchon's magnum opus, I wish to suggest, grandiosely announces the failure of that project of historiographical justice—at least as it stands conceived in the letter to Hirsch. "Pynchon's project is not primarily a reconstruction of history from the point of view of its victims," and "he works to decentre the possibility of an established authoritative objective account of historical events" (Holton 340). The evidence suggests, especially in relation to *V.*, that that stance is not a theoretical position held a priori but one that he develops from working with the archive and experiencing the difficulties of revision. I wish then to ask, examining two instances of Pynchon's use of documentary sources in "Mondaugen's story," chapter 9 of *V.*, whether or not the failure of his ethicohistorical project was inevitable. (...)

In this essay, examining Pynchon's "sources" has not simply produced the pleasure of discovery and of locating the points at which he differs from and revises the "original" writers' interpretation of events (Steenkamp in *Gravity's Rainbow*, the 1923 *Report* in *V.*, for instance), but has happened upon a point at which no specific interpretation is proffered by the source; the account is left to shock and fascinate on its own with no interpretation much more plausible than another. Thomas Pynchon, in a spirit of critique, proffers an account of his own, interpreting nevertheless, whether, writing the chapter, he had been attentive to all of the enigmas of this nearly forgotten "source" or not. Like the Bondel's song, which is sung but not understood, reading the source carefully warns us against interpretation itself and the tendency to indulge in hasty historical revisionism, although, of course, it would indeed be making an interpretation to say that in this case, there may not be an interpretation, although various interpretations can be *made*.

—Mark Sanders, "The Politics of Literary Reinscription in Thomas Pynchon's *V.*" *Critique: Studies in Contemporary Fiction* 39, no. 1 (1997): 81–82, 95.

MARK D. HAWTHORNE ON THE CREATION AND EFFECTS OF GENDER AND GENDER ROLES

[Mark D. Hawthorne is Professor of Technical and Scientific Communication at James Madison University, where he currently teaches web design, applied ethics, and on-line documentation. He has written extensively on Beckett, Pynchon, Kosinski, and Coetzee. In this piece, Hawthorne argues that distinguishing between a biological definition of *sex* and a social construction of *gender* helps readers to more fully understand the nature of *V.*]

Published ten years after the second of the Kinsey Reports (1948, 1953), the same year as Betty Friedan's *The Feminine Mystique*, two years before the founding of NOW, and almost a decade before the Gay Liberation Movement, Thomas Pynchon's *V.* (1963) stands at a pivotal moment in the construction of modern American sexuality and sex role identification. Although Mary Allen examined the "blankness" of women in *V.* and aptly concluded that "the variety of women in *V.* results from the various fantasies of men" and Alice Jardine clearly showed that "V. herself is nothing more than a 'fetish-construction' ... [that] Man will always search for, without ever knowing why," neither study also considered the way(s) in which Man, masculinity, and maleness are also social constructions that shape, and are shaped by, the feminine. While I do not want to displace these earlier, specifically feminist, readings, I do hope to suggest that the time is ripe to augment them. In other words, *V.* needs to be (re)read from the vantage of its pervasive sexuality or treatment of gender roles and gender identification.

Despite Hanjo Berressem's intriguing reading of the fetish in *V.* through insights derived from Freudian and Lacanian psychoanalysis, Pynchon's analysis of sex and gender directly owes little to sexology or psychoanalysis. After a pseudo-explanation of V.'s lesbianism in Paris toys with Freud's early (1911) concept of homosexuality as narcissism, Stencil summarily distances himself from this explanation by concluding, "her preferences *merely* lay outside the usual, exogamous-heterosexual pattern which prevailed in 1913," the insertion of "merely" suggesting, I think, his impatient disdain. Such disdain reflects a 1950s discourse on gender and sexuality. For example, as late as 1976, David and Brannon in their major review of the sociological literature on gender differentiation found that they could locate no book then in print that specifically treated the male sex role. Looking back on his Cornell days, Pynchon himself commented that "1958 ... was another planet. You have to appreciate the extent of sexual repression on that campus at the time." Because he seems to have little or no formal underpinning for his views on sex role identity, we might find Pynchon's attitudes at times naive, uninformed, or even crude after the impact of feminism, of the male and gay liberation movements, and of Political Correctness, but in the context of the late 50s and early 60s they are both enlightened and radical. If he privileges phallocentricity, he ridicules the assumption and arrogance of male domination; if he privileges male homosocial at the expense of heterosocial bonding, and thus frequently seems to denigrate the feminine, he avoids the sorts of homophobia classically defined by Gregory Lehne as a "characteristic of individuals who are generally rigid and sexist" or by Stephen Morin and Ellen Garfinkle as the sort of fear that heterosexual men may have of "their own sexual impulses toward men." Despite Catherine Stimpson's early feminist confusion of homosexuality and sadism, a reading of *V.* by way of Norman Mailer, his almost silent use of male homosexuality is shocking— even, I suggest, loud—when we place it against his structural use of the gay bar in *Lot 49* and anal sodomy in *Gravity's Rainbow*.

Eve Sedgwick demarcates biological "sex" as "chromosomal sex" and the meaning of "gender" as "culturally mutable and variable, highly relational, ... and inextricable from a history of power differential between gender." In her textbook definition, Susan Basow simplifies that "*Sex* is a biological term; people are termed either male or female depending on their sex organs and genes. In contrast, *gender* is a psychological and cultural term, referring to one's subjective feelings of maleness or femaleness (*gender identity*)." At no point in *V.* do we question V.'s biological sex, though in "V. in Love" and in her role as The Bad Priest, Stencil and Fausto identify her with masculine gender or sex role identity. Likewise, Pynchon never allows us to doubt Profane's biological maleness, though he constructs Profane's behavior to contrast the socially and psychoanalytically defined male gender identity of the 1950s.

Thus if we assume a constructionist view of gender and read Benny in the context of the 1950s, we can more closely focus on the attempts of the narrator(s) and Stencil to construct gender behavior opposed to, or deviating from, what Joseph Pleck calls "sex role stereotypes" and "sex role norms," culturally shared beliefs about what the sexes descriptively are and prescriptively believe they should be. The obviously male and masculine Stencil sets V.'s struggle to reject phallocentricity against a political discourse that, in turn, shaped twentieth-century sexuality; thus I agree with Alice Jardine's ahistorical reading of V. as "the space of slippage, the spaces of non-resemblance, within the sign, among the signifier, signified, and referent," though I will also argue that we must refer this space to the specifically masculine voice that has constructed his narration within historical boundaries that we are not allowed to forget or ignore (e.g., Egypt in 1898, Florence in 1899, Paris in 1913, or South-West Africa in 1922—all conceived from Stencil's vantage of 1956). Set in the sexual confusion of the 1950s and thus preceding Feminism's attempts to (re)define gender, the main narrator feminizes Benny when we measure him by either David and Brannon's "four basic themes which pervade and ultimately define the male sex role"—"No Sissy Stuff," "The Big Wheel," "The Sturdy Oak," and "Give 'Em Hell"—or Pleck's identification and analysis of a male sex role identity paradigm. In other words, V., as constructed by Stencil, and Profane, as constructed by the main narrator, are "people [who] indisputably belong to one sex and identify themselves as belonging to the corresponding gender while exhibiting a complex mixture of characteristics from each of the two standard gender roles"; without undue distortion, we can read them in the 1990s as "gender blenders."

—Mark D. Hawthorne, "A 'Hermaphrodite Sort of Deity': Sexuality, Gender, and Gender Blending in Thomas Pynchon's V." *Studies in the Novel* 29, no. 1 (1997): 74–76.

Melvyn New on the Examination of the Processes of Criticism

[Melvyn New is a Professor of English at the University of Florida. A specialist in eighteenth-century English literature and in the works of Sterne, he is the author of

Laurence Sterne as Satirist, Telling New Lies: Essays in Fiction, Past and Present, and *"Tristram Shandy": A Book for Free Spirits.* In this essay he demonstrates the ways in which *V.* charts two distinct critical ways of reading: one of which finds texts to be ultimately fragmented, and another which seeks to unify even the most fragmented text into a coherent whole.]

Pynchon's *V.* leads one quite readily into an examination of the critical process because it is so profoundly concerned with the human need to order fragments. While Herbert Stencil searches for clues to the meaning of the woman V., accumulating his notecards, his sources, his linkages, we, as readers, parallel his activity, making our own accumulations, driven by the same urge to fit the pieces together, to arrive at the meaning of the novel *V.* Other critics have noted this parallel, including Richard Poirier, who asks at one point, "What are critics of Pynchon, like myself, but a species of sorting demon?" On the other hand, Tony Tanner, the best critic thus far of Pynchon, is also correct in seeing Stencil as a surrogate author:

> One aspect of paranoia is the tendency to imagine plots around you; this is also the novelist's occupation and there is clearly a relationship between making fictions and imagining conspiracies.... [Stencil] is the man who is trying to make the connections and links, and put together the story which might well have been Pynchon's novel.
>
> *(City of Words)*

Without doubt, both author and critic have traditionally been makers of plots, the one imitating a scene which reflected transcendent order and pattern, the other tracing (that is, stenciling) that reflection of transcendence within the imitation. We are reminded of Pope's embodiment of this particular vision of the world: "A mighty maze, but not without a plan," and surely the primary aim of artist and reader prior to Pope was to explain, to defend, to justify that plan. But Pope had written an earlier version of the line, far more apropos to the twentieth century that Pynchon and Tanner are writing about: "A mighty maze of walks," Pope first wrote, "without a plan." For Northrop Frye the two versions embody a fundamental clash between life and art, but one reconciled by art:

> The first version recognizes the human situation; the second refers to the constructs of religion, art, and science that man throws up because he finds the recognition intolerable. Literature is an aspect of the human compulsion to create in the face of chaos. Romance, I think, is not only central to literature as a whole, but the area where we can see most clearly that the maze without a plan and the maze not without a plan are two aspects of the same thing.
>
> (*The Secular Scripture*)

For Pynchon, as for many twentieth-century writers, the problem is not quite as simple as Frye suggests, primarily because the modern awareness that the constructs may well be only constructs and nothing more returns the human situation to intolerableness. The human compulsion to create may indeed be, as we suspect in Stencil's case, a paranoid activity, a failure rather than an achievement of human intellect. (...)

The characters in *V.* are defined or define themselves in relation to certain private constructs, all of which share in Pynchon's overarching construct of an entropic progress from animateness in inanimateness, from life to annihilation. Because Pynchon builds an historical perspective into his pattern, there develops as well a series of legatorial relationships that penetrate the private constructs and perhaps serve as one hopeful signpost in an otherwise bleak landscape. Every construct except one, Victoria's relationship with Mélanie, is created by a male and embodies a female, usually—but not solely—associated with the ubiquitous letter V. Finally, and most obviously, Pynchon divides his world into past and future, the foreign-service world of stenciled plots and counterplots, and the nautical world (including the Whole Sick Crew) of Benny Profane, adrift in the "dreamscape of the future." Pynchon had worked with a similar division in his first published story, "Entropy," and he returns to its images late in *V.*:

"If there is any political moral to be found in this world," Stencil once wrote in his journal, "it is that we carry on the business of this century with an intolerable double vision. Right and Left; the hothouse and the street. The Right can only live and work hermetically, in the hothouse of the past, while outside the Left prosecute their affairs in the streets by manipulated mob violence. And cannot live but in the dreamscape of the future." (...)

It would probably not do to allegorize Pynchon, but the temptation is strong. Like Godolphin, we would like to impose our own "dream of order" on the ever-moving surface of *V.*, for like Vheissu, *V.* and all significant literary works can be considered a tattooed woman whose mystery we are driven to penetrate and possess. On one level, criticism is simply that process: we tear the work of art into its constituent elements, we delve below the surface (one of criticism's favorite metaphors) to the meaning supposedly hiding beneath the words or colors of shapes of the skin. But the process is always and necessarily unsatisfactory and incomplete: it is destructive, as is the love relationship in which the loved object is sacrificed to the needs of the lover. In the worlds of past and future this is perhaps all there is, and Pynchon mirrors this sacrifice in the various love relationships in *V.*, culminating in the sexual impalement of Mélanie, V.'s own object of love.

If there were nothing more, Pynchon's outlook would be bleak indeed.

> —Melvyn New, "Profaned and Stenciled Texts: In Search of Pynchon's V." *Thomas Pynchon: Modern Critical Views*, edited by Harold Bloom, (New York: Chelsea House, 1986): 97–98, 99, 102.

Deborah L. Madsen on the Elusiveness and Allusiveness of V.

[Deborah L. Madsen is Professor of English and Research Coordinator for the English Division at South

Bank University in London. A specialist in American Literature, she has published *American Exceptionalism, Beyond the Commonwealth: Expanding the Postcolonial Canon*, and *The Postmodernist Allegories of Thomas Pynchon*. In this chapter from her book on Pynchon, she examines ways in which V.'s elusiveness mirrors the decentered position of power in our age.]

The very title of *V* evokes the question: what or who is V? Although it is not formulated until much later, this problem forms the exegetical context for the entire narrative. It 'frames' the opening scene, set in Virginia, in the vicinity of the 'Sailor's Grave' where, 'overhead, turning everybody's face green and ugly, shone mercury-vapor lights, receding in an asymmetric V to the east where it's dark and there are no more bars'.[1] It is through such a street, illuminated by V—'the street of the twentieth century' (p. 323)—that the quest for 'her' significance leads. V exists as a narrative; as an historical figure, the Lady V; and as a proliferating number of V-structures or V-signs which are perceptible in the narrative world, such as these V-lights. The three elements share a common basis in the quest for V, for the genesis or etiology of the twentieth century—for its presiding genius.

The narrative and the quest are virtually identical, united in the attempt to discover the meaning and history of V through the temporal manifestations of the Lady V and of seemingly incidental V-signs. But the relationship is one of only virtual identity. A rhetorical gap is sustained between the two 'texts' so that whilst a character like Hugh Godolphin or Raphael Mantissa may conceive of V—as Vheissu or Venus—as a type of void, a 'gaudy dream, a dream of annihilation', the ongoing development of the narrative plot is directed towards the construction of a figural system in which V is the primary object of interpretation. The narrative attempts to discover the significance of the past for the present by bringing the two into a hermeneutic relationship with V. So whilst many of its characters are left vacillating in an existential void, the narrative itself attempts to vivify its verbal signs, to discover amid the various significations of V a signifying centre which would be the 'spirit' informing modern history, giving it pattern, significance and direction.

Like the 'Street', V's status is that of a metaphor. However, the 'tenors' to the 'vehicle' that is V are so various, their ontological and epistemological status so ambiguous and their relationship so disjunctive, as to suggest that the source of narrative uncertainty is located in the nature and function of V. For the uncertain status of V is a result of 'her' function, which is curiously akin to that of a personification figure. In V the signifier and the signified are so closely identified as to become one, so that 'she' becomes almost purely a signifier, and throughout the narrative the range of signification of this initial sign is explored in a number of contexts and through different interpretative structures. The identification of many V-figures gives rise to the possibility that together these figures constitute some kind of V-metaphysic, the *weltanschauung* of the twentieth century and modernity's link with the past. (...)

Stencil refuses to formulate a definition of V. His refusal to do so is based upon fear; fear that the 'sense of animateness' he discovers through the quest will disappear with its conclusion; the fear that it will be revealed as a consequence of Stencil's own determination by the cultural discourses represented by V.

A provisional movement towards closure, towards defining the ontological nature of V, is made in the Epilogue. Here, the narrative approaches V more closely than Stencil ever dares, through the point of view of Sidney Stencil; and likewise, those concepts that characterize the V-metaphysic are brought into a closer conjunction. Particularly, the nature of history as metaphor and its relation to the pretextual status of the V-metaphysic are discussed in explicit terms. The sailor Mehmet, for instance, claims that the world, like th eindividual, is dying of old age; that all change tends in the direction of death, in a constant progression of decay, and that civilization and the crises of politics simply disguise this inexorable process. It is Sidney Stencil, however, who casts this development in terms of an historical principle: 'suppose instead sometime between 1859 and 1919, the world contracted a disease which no one ever took the trouble to diagnose because the symptoms were too subtle—blending in with the events of history, no different one by one but altogether fatal' (p.461). David Richter has identified the significance of 1859 as the year in which both Marx's *Critique of Political Economy* and Darwin's *The Origin of Species* were published thus making the inception of a mechanistic image of man and society. This world view characterizes all of V's figural manifestations.

Stencil continues to see the marks of this disease, old age or V-metaphysic manifest in the world around him. Consequently, he develops an apocalyptic attitude towards history, particularly in terms of the involvement of the Catholic Church in political crises.

> She awaited a Third Kingdom. Violent overthrow is a Christian phenomenon.
> The matter of a Paraclete's coming, the comforter, the dove; the tongues of flame, the gift of tongues: Pentecost, Third person of the Trinity. None of it was implausible to Stencil. The Father had come and gone. In political terms, the Father was the Prince ; the single leader, the dynamic figure whose virtú used to be a determinant of history. This had denigrated to the Son, genius of the liberal love-feast which had produced 1848 and lately the overthrow of the Czars. What next? What Apocalypse?
> Especially on Malta, a matriarchal island. Would the Paraclete be also a mother? Comforter, true. But what gift of communication could ever come from a woman ... (p. 472).

Stencil adopts Joachim of Flora's millennial prediction of an Age of Grace, the Age of the Holy Ghost, which would supersede the Age of the Sone, to summarize the development of V from 'virgin' working through faith; to 'bride' and incorporating the element of virtú, which Victoria Wren had hoped would be a 'determinant of history'; to 'Mother' and 'Queen'.

In this connection, Stencil suggests an analogy between V and the goddess Mara. Like Astarte, the figure-head of Mehemet's xebec, Mara is a goddess of love and death, related to V through her association with Venus; 'disguise is one of her attributes'; and though 'she once had access to the entire island and the waters as far as the fishing banks off Lampedusa' (pp. 461–62), she is constrained to haunt Xaghriet Mewwija, on which Valletta is situated. The most conclusive evidence for a definitive link between V and Mara is the circumstance of Stencil's death. Having surrendered himself to Victoria/Veronica, he nonetheless leaves Malta, aboard Mehemet's xebec. But V's latest conquest does not proceed past the limit of Mara's domain 'the invisible circle centred at Xaghriet Mewwija with Lampedusa on the rim' (p. 462). Perhaps a victim of accident, still Stencil is prevented from ever revealing the nature of V, such as he knows it.

The narrative approaches the question no closer. The dual function of V as both *figura* and allegoric pretext prevents the totalization of meaning because V represents only fragmentary aspects of a total pretextual discourse. Though V works through the conquering of individual minds, this subjective dissolution of meaning prevents the certain identification of any transhistorical force. The determination of personal identity by the kind of powerful cultural discourse that V (as *figura*) represents works to constrain the interpretation of history to a single channel even as it multiplies the 'histories' according to the number of its interpreters. For whilst the allegoric quester discovers that the questing self is the product of the same set of beliefs and values that is represented by allegoric *figurae*, and the allegoric pretext, the subject and object of interpretation merge in such a way that no significant discovery concerning the nature of culture can be made. For as long as V represents the dominant epistemologies made available by the narrative's pretext and also represents the determination of the protagonists' subjectivities then the meaning of history will remain trapped within a hermeneutic circle. However, postmodernist allegories, such as *V*, suggest that this is an intended consequence of the ideological circumscription of social knowledge, for in this way the real centres of power, of economic and political power, remain unidentified and unfettered. For those who are kept in a condition of ignorance, subject to the tyranny of the signifier, this cultural power base will be represented only as that which cannot be represented, as that which remains hidden: the absent centre to which all things tend.

NOTES

1. Thomas Pynchon, *V* (1963, rpt., London: Picador, 1978), p. 10. Future references are given in the text.

—Deborah L. Madsen, "Vacillating in the Void? Verbal Vivication in *V.*" in *The Postmodernist Allegories of Thomas Pynchon*, (New York: St. Martin's, 1991): 29–30, 50–52.

JOSEPHINE HENDIN ON THE FIGURE OF DEATH

[Josephine Hendin is Professor of English at New York University. Her books include *The Right Thing to Do*, *The Feminist Press*, *The World of Flannery O'Connor* and *Vulnerable People*. Here, Hendin shows that the genius of Pynchon and *V.* comes through their rejection of the concept of salvation in the face of destruction and death.]

Thomas Pynchon knows the high cost of living better than anybody except the devil. Pynchon is the evil genius of our time, the man with the quickest eye for what makes this an age of rapacity and sexual hate. He is the American Goya whose dazzling canvases are lit from hell, whose message is: Death Rules.

The dream of this age is the dream of vulnerability conquered. Pynchon's first novel put life together as a diabolic pact in which you could trade your soul for insurance against hell on earth. At twenty-five he dared to say that what his generation required was salvation from death *and* life. His novel *V.* showed the way to eternal experience without anger, pain, or fear. Published in 1963, it was set in 1955 because the Cold War was an unbeatable image for the standoff between Eros and Thanatos in suburban marriages, in New York games of musical blankets, for the deadlock whose linear representation was the symmetrical letter

V. Pynchon saw the freeze as an emotional necessity. He wrote about people who knew that love could not diminish suffering because it was love that produced half the anguish there was. He knew what the world wanted was not another Christ but an end to the daily passion play.

Pynchon's symbol for human salvation was not the cross but the partridge in the pear tree: the bird lives off the pears; his droppings fertilize the tree so it can make more pears; the bird makes more droppings. Nature is a Newtonian motion machine powered by crap. Among people, too, salvation is symbiosis. The prime mover shows you how to keep it going without upsetting the bird! Pynchon's Christmas present to his generation was the God who was a birdbrain machine. (…)

Technology is commonly blamed as the source of all our woes, our short-circuited relations, our IBMized lives. But many people envy machines. Pynchon loves and hates his messiah machine in *V.*, Benny Profane, a man whose nightmare is that his "clock-heart" and "sponge" brain will be disassembled on the rubble-strewn streets, but whose grace is his ability to be a perpetual-motion man who rolls on too fast to lose his heart or let anyone touch the controls of his mind. The profane Christ is the one who won't get crucified.

Profane's world is no vale of tears. His nativity is one Christmas Eve in the Sailor's Grave Bar, the hip world where every man's a drunken sailor, and women are interchangeable quick lays. Everyone's waiting for Suck Hour, the moment when Chow Down calls the sailors to custom beer taps made of foam rubber in the shape of large breasts. There were seven taps and an average of 250 sailors diving to be given suck by a beer-breast. There's very little nourishment in Pynchon's world. His wise man controls his thirsts. Profane does not really want to turn on anything, even a beer tap. He wants a woman who will not love him but be a really self-contained machine: "Any problems with her you could look up in a maintenance manual. Remove and replace was all." He gets an erection thinking about the sex money can buy while reading the want ads, and notices his erection traces a line in the *Times*. But he waits until it subsides so he can choose the agency where it comes to rest. He wants the least exciting job. He has the peace that passeth understanding.

History produced this human yo-yo. The profane light began with the Victorians' penetration of darkness. Pynchon's favorite explorer, Godolphin, went to Africa to civilize the natives and discovered the cannibal in himself, the need to murder the beauty whose sexual pull made him want to mutilate her. In a spectacular scene he flees to the South Pole and finds, while digging a hole to plant the British flag and reassert his arctic respectability, an African spider monkey all tail, clutch, and cling. The heat of sex is connected with the ice of death. Does one lead to the other because intimacy kills? Realizing he will never escape the destructiveness in himself, the explorer embodies civilization's crucial question: how to keep the monkey off your back?

The history of male striving for control can be written in excrement, as Norman O. Brown implied. Pynchon wrote it in his wacky sewer scenes where evil is the devil you can't flush any further away. Three of *V.*'s characters descend into the urban colon. A Victorian priest preaches in the sewers of New York because he sees people as rats trying to become sanctified. He and his generation could still believe rats had souls. A middle-aged man goes through the sewer looking for clues to his mother, V., because life is possible for him only as the endless romantic quest that keeps him too busy to notice the stench. Young Profane is on the sewer patrol just to earn the money for women and food. He embraces his meaninglessness as a value. He makes the directionless flow of crap his life.

V. herself is female serenity, the clean, eternal balance of emotional control. She absorbs the force of war, of all male thrusts, as erotic curios, and returns them when as mother she abandons, as protectress she corrupts, as lover she murders, as transvestite priest she damns. She is the destructive, indestructible objet d'art who mutilates her body to adorn it with golden feet and a glass eye. She is always young, always fascinatingly beautiful. One man dreams of her ecstatically as a young machine: "At age 76, skin radiant with the bloom of some new plastic, both eyes glass, but now containing photoelectric cells connected by silver electrodes to optic nerves.... Perhaps even a complex system of pressure transducers located in a marvelous vagina of polyethylene, all leading to a single silver cable which fed pleasure voltages direct to the correct register of the digital machine in her skull." She is Profane's woman, the girl who has lost her virginity to the gear shift of her MG, whose great love is her car or its human equivalent, Profane. V. is a self-contained autoerotic machine. V. is the crucial pivot, the profane fulcrum on which you can survive forever. V. is vulnerability conquered.

Life is best as a machine! The degree to which men and women want each other to be ever-ready erotic tools, needing neither tenderness nor love, is one sign of sexual hate. Pynchon is saying that men control their destructiveness through Profane-like passivity and disengagement; that women conquer their vulnerability to men, life, and death by becoming virtual automatons who cannot feel a thing. "Keep cool, but care," someone advises. The only way to contain your destructiveness is to deadlock the two, to be the partridge and pear tree locked in endless, profane life, forever content.

"O trees of life, when will your winter come?" asked Rilke. For Pynchon winter came somewhere between *V.* and *Gravity's Rainbow*. Pynchon stopped playing the V. game, stopped telling us how to survive. He broke the balance of *V.*, released the deadlock between destructiveness and control, melted the Cold War into an open battle in which the rats surfaced, and violence broke free for a war between life and death. Death won. Pynchon became the devil, the fantasist whose rainbow has its origin in gravity, the spirit of the down. *Gravity's Rainbow* is death's fantasy that life exists. (...)

Pynchon is the devil who went beyond the grave to anatomize the remains of the modern soul. Like Death himself he is the ultimate collector, putting together the emotional, cultural, and historical life of his generation with a brilliance and depth that outstrips in scope what Thomas Mann did for the prewar world in *The Magic Mountain*, that equals James Joyce's compendium of his time in *Ulysses*. He plays Beethoven to Rilke's Schubert, developing from Rilke's encapsulated emotional statements operative definitions about the nature of science, thought, and civilization. Pynchon is quite simply the genius of his generation. He is the Antichrist who offered up his own destructiveness to illuminate yours. Pynchon is the one man who realized that the moralist of our time would have to be the devil.

—Josephine Hendin, "What is Thomas Pynchon Telling Us?" *Harpers* 250 no. 1498 (March, 1975): 37–39.

PLOT SUMMARY OF
Gravity's Rainbow

Even more so than for *V.*, a summary of *Gravity's Rainbow*—because of the size, breadth, and sheer amount of information and characters as well as the fact that much of what "happens" in the novel takes place in dreams, fantasy, speculation, faulty memories, and vastly separated time periods—is exceedingly difficult and not particularly useful. So much of the novel's contents, its events and people, must be left out; what remains constitutes at most a hastily drawn map of a strange, unexplored country—or what is perhaps more appropriate, a faded print of an old film that has most likely been repaired and spliced together incorrectly. Nevertheless, certain large structures within the book stand out, and a familiarity with them will certainly help the reader to navigate through this land and to understand the "film" on the screen. In its simplest sense, the novel is divided into four major sections, and the following summary attempts to give the main events and ideas form.

Part 1: Beyond the Zero

At the start of the novel "a screaming comes across the sky": it is 1944, late in the Second World War, and a German V-2 rocket is heading towards London. From the banana garden on his roof, Captain Pirate Prentice watches its trail rise in the sky then disappear. The rocket has spent all its fuel, he realizes, and it is now coasting towards its target: "incoming mail," Prentice describes it to himself. Prentice muses on the dreadful silence of the rocket as compared to traditional bombing raids: because the V-2 travels faster than the speed of sound, the first thing one hears is not the rocket itself but the explosion it causes. Only after it explodes does the sound of the rocket approaching catch up to the listener.

Returning downstairs to fix one of his famous banana breakfasts, Prentice wonders why he hasn't heard the explosion of the rocket and decides that it must haven fallen short of its target and crashed into the sea. But he receives word that the rocket did indeed crash in London and contained not a bomb but a message for Prentice himself. He leaves to retrieve the message (which is written in a type of invisible ink called kryptosam—and which can only be made visible by the application of Prentice's own semen), and we then meet the novel's "central" character, Tyrone Slothrop, an American stationed in London.

Slothrop, the descendant of an old New England family of failures, was as an infant the subject of behaviorist experiments at Harvard by one Lazlo Jamf. Through these experiments, infant Slothrop was conditioned to have an erection when in the presence of a stimulus which for the time being is unnamed. Over Slothrop's desk hangs a map of London, dotted with stars in seemingly random locations.

Two other important characters are soon introduced: the lovers Roger Mexico and Jessica Swanlake. Mexico is a statistician who also has a map of London dotted with stars. The starred locations on Mexico's map follow the Poisson distribution mathematically, but physically they chart the locations where V-2s have exploded in London. Later we learn that Mexico and Slothrop's map are identical, although the points on Slothrop's represent the places where he has had sex. Furthermore, Slothrop's conquests always predate the rocket impacts by a statistically meaningful time period. The strangeness of this almost impossible coincidence prompts a significant question: is Slothrop somehow predicting the site of the V-2 explosions or is he somehow luring the rockets to these locations, that is, somehow causing them?

Also on the scene is Mexico's boss at the "White Visitation," Ned Pointsman—a mad scientist obsessed with Pavlovian studies on humans—and Pointsman's boss, Brigadier Pudding. The White Visitation is a former mental hospital that been taken over for military purposes. Also part of the military's plans is "Operation Blackwing," a psychological attack on Germany, specifically on the German's racial fears of the hereros—Africans whom the Germans eradicated earlier in the century. Blackwing's purpose is to fashion evidence of a fictional "Schwarzkommando" resistance unit operating underground in Germany.

The reader also encounters Pirate's operative, Katje Borgesius, who recalls her former assignment in Holland with Gottfried and Captain Blicero—who appears in *V.* as Lt. Weissman. While Weissman/Blicero recalls the Enzian, the Herero boy who is also his lover, and Slothrop is sent off on a mission to the Riviera, Grigori the octopus is shown a film of Katje so that he will recognize her later.

Part 2: Un Perm'au Casino Hermann Goering

Slothrop wakes in a room at the Casino Hermann Goering on the Riviera and meets two other operatives from London, Tantivy Mucker-Maffick and Teddy Bloat. Heading to the beach for a picnic, Slothrop sees a girl in the water being attacked by an octopus: all part of the White Visitations experiment with and on Slothrop, the girl is Katje and the octopus Grigori. Slothrop saves Katje with a crab, but begins to feel that forces are manipulating him beyond his control. After a night of sex and seltzer fights with Katje, Slothrop awakens to find his clothes and identification cards stolen. Without a real identity now, and left alone with Katje, Slothrop's paranoia overwhelms him, giving him his first glimpse of a group of oppressors he can only name "Them." Later, after Katje has vanished, Slothrop begins to study plans for the V-2 and stumbles across some very interesting information about the rocket's construction—and one odd side effect: when he reads the plans he finds they cause him to have an erection.

Meanwhile, back at the White Visitation, Katje has returned in the guise of a dominatrix to make sure that Brigadier Pudding—who is in charge of funding the project—remains under Pointsman's control. In a scene that recalls the graphic, almost pornographic, nose job in *V.*, we see the tryst between Pudding and Katje as "mistress of the night," in which Pudding eats her feces—his way of dealing with the death and destruction he witnessed in the First World War.

Back on the Riviera, Slothrop discovers disturbing evidence of connections between Allied and German industries such as IG Farben and Shell Oil—connections which only further intensify his paranoia—he begins to develop several "Proverbs for Paranoids"—and his sense of the oppressiveness of "Them." Continuing to study the German rocket plans, Slothrop also first reads of "Imipolex G," a plastic whose nature and use will soon figure prominently in the novel.

At Raoul's raucous party, Slothrop meets Blodgett Waxwing, who wears a white zoot suit. Waxwing tells Slothrop of an insidious plot that is behind the supposed rescue of Katje from the octopus, but he is unable to supply Slothrop with much in the way of specific information. Waxwing also gives Slothrop a business card and a zoot suit owned by a former victim of the Zoot Suit Riots of Los Angeles in 1943, then disappears, his primary talent being the ability to fade out whenever he wants to.

As it turns out, Imipolex G is nothing more menacing than a new plastic—but one developed by Lazlo Jamf for IG Farben based on research done earlier at DuPont. After a history both of the development of plastics and the development of the corporations that invented them, Slothrop comes across a reference in the rocket plans to "S-Gerät, 11/00000," a special model V-2 rocket that includes as part of its construction the sinister Imipolex G. After he learns of the possibly faked "honorable death" of his friend Tantivy, Slothrop escapes to Nice, to track down the address on the card given him by Waxwing. In Nice, he acquires a new name and identity cards and sets off for Zurich as Ian Scuffling. In Zurich he realizes that there is no returning to anything in store for him, and after pawning his zoot suit and wandering through the city, he bounces between Zurich and Geneva, hoping to acquire more information on the S-great and the plot.

As the action shifts once more to the White Visitation, we learn that Intelligence has "lost" Slothrop and the supposed connection between Mexico and Slothrop's map may not exist: there is no evidence that any of Slothrop's "scores" in London ever took place. The war ends, but as Pointsman begins to wonder about taking apart his organization and as he begins to hear voices in his head, it is revealed that there really is a Schwarzkommando rocket troop in Germany.

Part 3: In the Zone

The war is over but the Post-War—unlike the term *postwar*, which refers to a time of peace after a war is over, the Post-War is a period in which the war continues but under different or even hidden terms—rages on in the Zone, an unidentified and barren land in which oppression is the key principle. Slothrop/Scuffling is still hunting for the mysterious S-Gërat, the 00000 V-2 rocket, but as in so much of Pynchon's work, the more information he finds, the less clear things become. On the train to Nordhausen, Slothrop learns more about his past as an experimental subject: his father had leased him to Jam in order to send him to college. The experiment itself evidently involved stimulus by Imipolex G to produce an erection—a result which is evident even as Slothrop simply remembers the smell itself. Also on the train are the fictitious/real African rocket troops, the Schwarzkommando, who are also looking for the 00000 rocket. Later, after meeting Geli Tripping, Slothrop learns of the even more mysterious black device, the Schwarzgerät.

At the Mittelwerke Slothrop encounters the Schwarzkommando and learns the story of both the Zone Hereros—the "Erdschweinhöhle" whose motto is "I am passed over"—and of Enzian, half-brother of the Russian, Tchitcherine, who is more metal than human.

Back in Berlin, Slothrop/Scuffling takes on his next guise— Rocketman!—and at a gangster bar, he encounters the sailor from *V.*, Seaman Bodine, who sends Rocketman on a drug-hunting expedition. After hearing of Roosevelt's death and taking on another new/additional identity (Max Schlepzig), he goes to retrieve Bodine's buried hashish, only to encounter Mickey Rooney! After this strange encounter, Rocketman is captured, then released (and trailed) by Tchitcherine, who is also interested in the 00000 and the S-Great. Rocketman meets up with the actress Greta Erdmann, who is searching for her daughter Bianca, who was conceived during the filming of a movie with the "real" Max Schlepzig, another actor—a scene which Slothrop/Rocketman/Schlepzig recreates on the movie set with Greta.

Rocketman and Greta reach Bad Karma, still searching for the 00000 and Bianca. On board the yacht *Anubis* after nearly drowning, Slothrop meets Bianca, a twelve-year-old "knockout," with whom he later has sex. Believing that Bianca has jumped overboard, Slothrop follows and is rescued by one Frau Gnahb, who takes him Swinemünde. There, during a raid on a Russian compound, Slothrop begins to "thin, to scatter."

As the action turns yet again to the White Visitation, we learn of Pudding's death—of an *E. coli* infection he caught from eating Katje's feces. Katje, meanwhile, visits Pirate Prentice's, where she learns of a "counterforce" forming to undo the work of Pointsman and others.

After raiding a deserted Schwarzkommando camp, Tchitcherine discovers more information on the "Schwarzgerät" and encounters Slothrop, whom he mistakes for a Russian intelligence officer. Slothrop, meanwhile, meets a group of children who ask him to play the role of the "pig hero" in their town festival. Later, dressed in a pig costume and after a daring escape with another pig, Slothrop meets Pokler, who presumably knows much about the Schwarzgerat. Again on the run from the police in the pig suit, Slothrop meets up with Seaman Bodine. Exchanging clothes in a brothel with his nemesis Marvy, Slothrop-Marvy escapes, while Marvy-Pig is captured as Slothrop and by Pointsman's orders is mistakenly castrated.

Part 4: The Counterforce

Actresses Bette Davis and Margaret Dumont, with Slothrop nearby, hear what they think is a very loud kazoo but what is really Pirate Prentice in a pirated P-47 Thunderbolt flying overhead. Prentice—as well as many others—is searching for Slothrop, but there may not be much left of him to be found. Wandering through the Zone, Slothrop finds the harmonica he lost years ago in Boston, and then he simply "disperses," scatters as a whole and unified person. Throughout the remainder of the novel, Slothrop appears in diffuse and disjointed form, most often as the sound of harmonica music playing somewhere unspecific.

In what may be a flashback or memory of Mexico's, we learn about the goals of the counterforce. Having lost Jessica, Mexico turned against Pointsman and joined Pirate. Prentice tells him of the need for a system or state of creative paranoia in which the authoritarian and oppressive "Them" is countered by an anarchic "Us." Even though Mexico believes this is exactly what "They" want "Us" to do, he agrees to join the counterforce.

One of the more cryptic sections of the final part of the novel is the story of "Byron the Bulb," an immortal lightbulb who (?) has already appeared several times earlier in the book. Byron has dreamed of defeating the international light-bulb cartel, but while he will go on burning forever, he can never achieve his goal. The best he can hope for is to know "the truth" of Them but be powerless to do anything about Them—which is perhaps the same than can be said for Prentice, Mexico, and the Counterforce.

Elsewhere, Katje meets Enzian and learns of the launch of the 00000 with Gottfried (the S-Gërat himself) selected by Weissmaan as its human payload. Katje also learns that the Schwarzkommando have assembled their own V-2, the 00001, from scavenged parts of other rockets left throughout the Zone and that they intend to fire it soon.

As for Slothrop, we are told that he "has become one plucked albatross ... scattered, all over the Zone. It's doubtful if he can ever be 'found' again." The last anyone sees of Slothrop is on the cover of an obscure sixties band, the Fool.

As the novel ends, scenes of Gottfried's launch in the 00000 are spliced with scenes from the Orpheus Theater in Los Angeles. As the rocket goes through its launch, ascent, and descent, the screen in the theater goes dark. While the disgruntled audience shouts for the show to begin, the rocket is falling "nearly a mile per second," towards the Orpheus. At the very end, we are told there is just enough time left to "touch the person next to you, or to reach between your own cold legs."

LIST OF CHARACTERS IN
Gravity's Rainbow

Out of the—literally—hundreds of characters in the novel, it is difficult if not perhaps impossible to list all of them concisely. The following list contains some of the more important, central, and interesting characters.

Geoffrey "Pirate" Prentice is a Captain in the British Army and works for Special Operations Executive or the "Firm." A dreamer who is able to get inside other people's fantasies, he is already at the beginning of the novel convinced that the war, which is nearly over, will be continued by a "Them" whose only purpose will be to use "Us" for their own increased profit. He becomes a member of the Counterforce, whose goal is to use creative paranoia to thwart "Them," even though they may actually be a construction *of* "Them."

The central and most important character in the novel, **Tyrone Slothrop** was the subject of behaviorist experiments as an infant. Trained by Lazlo Jamf to have an erection when in the presence of Imipolex G, Slothrop is also used as a guinea pig by various intelligence organizations on both "sides" of the war. A man of many guises, Slothrop "scatters" towards the end of the novel though he remains present as a kind of counterforce of his own.

Roger Mexico, one of Prentice's associates and "provisional" friends, is a mathematician and the "antiPointsman" who also is in love with Jessica Swanlake. His map of the V-2 explosions matches Slothrop's map of his sexual conquests. After he learns that Jessica actually works for Pointsman, Mexico decides, though not without reservation, to join the Counterforce.

More than any other single character the physical face of evil and "Them" in the novel, **Dr. Edward W. A. ("Ned") Pointsman** is a Pavlovian at the White Visitation. Using Slothrop as his "ticket" to the Nobel Prize, Pointsman is locked into a worldview where only one and zero exist, where only cause and effect rule. Functioning as the "antiMexico," he has started to go mad by the end of the novel's first section. Ultimately, he is in disgrace for the accidental castration of Marvy and receives an elaborate dressing-down from Mexico.

Old Brigadier **Ernest Pudding** is the aging World War I vet in charge of—though really at the mercy of—the White Visitation. Possibly senile and delusional at the best of times, he is kept in step by Pointsman, who sends him to meet Katje Borgesius in her guise as the Domina Nocturna. Although he dies of massive *E. coli* infection, he constitutes one of the ghost members of the Counterforce.

Katje Borgesius is an agent with no clear allegiances who first appears in the novel through her "kryptosam" message to Pirate. An "ice queen" who turned Jews over to the Nazis to remove suspicion from herself, Katje aids Pointsman in his experiment on Slothrop.

Captain/Major Weissmann, also called Blicero, was involved with both Katje and Gottfried in South-West Africa. A "part salesman, part scientist" who is ultimately in love with his own death, and described as "the Zone's worst specter," he chooses Gottfried to be sacrificed in the 00000 V-2.

Oberst Enzian, is the half-brother of Tchitcherine, the "monster" and protégé of Blicero, and one of the Herero "preterite," those who were passed over in the genocide of their nation. Ultimately leader of the Schwarzkommando and the divided Herero survivors, he is able to scrap together another V-2, the 00001.

Half brother to Enzian, **Vaslav Tchitcherine**, is the Soviet intelligence officer whose goal is to destroy the Schwarzkommando and to find out the truth about the 00000. He is also one of Geli Tripping's lover, and in the end he stays with her because of a spell she has cast over him.

Gottfried, called the "pet and protégé" of Blicero/Weissmann, is also the mysterious S-Gërat of rocket 00000: its human payload launched into space.

Margherita ("Greta") Erdmann is an actress in German films and the mother of Bianca. Another one of Slothrop's lovers, she is also connected to Blicero/Weissmann.

Bianca Erdmann, ostensibly the daughter of Greta Erdmann and Miklos Thanatz, is actually the daughter of the actor Max Schlepzig, and was conceived during a scene in one of her parents' movies. A "clever child" and yet another one of Slothrop's lovers, her dead body is discovered by Slothrop when he returns to the *Anubis*.

A one-time lover of Mexico, **Jessica Swanlake** is actually on the side of "Them" and works for Pointsman.

One of Slothrop's lovers and a witch-in-training, **Geli Tripping**, is also one of Tchitcherine's lovers.

A recurring character not only in *Gravity's Rainbow* but also in *V.* and, through his ancestor, in *Mason & Dixon* as well, **Seaman Bodine** is the rowdy, drug-running, drunkard and trickster who crosses paths several times with Slothrop.

Blodgett Waxwing is the zoot-suit-wearing forger of identity cards Slothrop meets at Raoul's party. He is gives Slothrop a zoot suit of his own as well as the identity of war correspondent Ian Scuffling.

CRITICAL VIEWS ON
Gravity's Rainbow

DAVID COWART ON THE IMPLICATIONS OF FILM AND CINEMA

[David Cowart is a Professor of English at the University of South Carolina. His books include *Literary Symbiosis: The Reconfigured Text in Twentieth-Century Writing, History and the Contemporary Novel, Arches and Light: The Fiction of John Gardner,* and *Thomas Pynchon: The Art of Allusion.* In this chapter from his Pynchon book, Cowart contends that in the novel Pynchon makes no significant distinctions between film and so-called real life.]

Pynchon's pictorial-allusive imagination, manifested in embryonic form in the first two novels, takes on a special importance in *Gravity's Rainbow*, where it gives rise to multiple references to and metaphors from the art of the cinema. These allusions are more prominent, hence of greater structural and thematic importance, than the Botticelli and Varo allusions of the previous novels. Characters in *V.* and *The Crying of Lot 49* discovered the basic thinness of life by looking at paintings. Their insight, into the illusory nature of reality, becomes more complex in *Gravity's Rainbow* because of the greater number of pictorial allusions in that book and because of the more lifelike, kinetic quality of the medium that furnishes them. Film's two-dimensionality is still emblematic of a superficiality in life itself, but now the interaction between that which is lived and that which is viewed is far more exciting and convoluted: as if the interplay between Oedipa Maas's education in what constitutes reality on the one hand, and Remedios Varo's pictorial representation of that reality and its relation to the individual mind on the other, were multiplied and refracted—as if *The Crying of Lot 49* were set entirely in an art museum: not "a gallery one is familiar with but long weary of" (*V.*, p. 160), but one "wandered into" (*The Crying of Lot 49*, p. 20), hence fresh and compelling to the eye and mind.

In each of the novels, to a greater or lesser extent, Pynchon concerns himself with the relationship between life and its two-dimensional imitation. If life is itself two-dimensional in a metaphysical sense—"cosmetics for the Void" was the nihilist formulation arrived at in the last chapter—can one regard it as more "real," more "true," than its pictorial counterfeit? The question presents itself most intriguingly when the "counterfeit" is film (which is so much more perceptibly lifelike than painting that the English called their first movie theatre "The Bioscope"). In *Gravity's Rainbow* Pynchon uses film as a critique of life, insisting that the one is not more or less real than the other. (...)

For those of us born since 1930 (Pynchon was born in 1937), the second world war exists almost exclusively as a film experience. We may have read a few books about it, but mostly we know it through newsreels, movies, and television documentaries like *The Twentieth Century* or *Victory at Sea*. Those who actually participated in the war may perceive it the same way, for in America and abroad movies were the preponderant source of popular entertainment before, during, and after the period of conflict. Such a pervasive cultural influence must naturally have influenced the way the war was perceived by soldier and civilian alike—just as it affects the way we look back on the war today.

Thus in addition to structuring his novel as a movie, Pynchon presents a narrator and characters who falter in their ability to distinguish between real life and movie life. When, for example, Slothrop's counterfeiting and dope-running friend Emil "Säure" Bummer informs him of Roosevelt's death, the American experiences an eerie moment in which he perceives the bombed-out city of Berlin as a tremendous movie set:

> Someone here is cleverly allowing for parallax, scaling, shadows all going the right way and lengthening with the day—but no, Säure can't. be real, no more than these dark-clothed extras waiting in queues for some hypothetical tram, some two slices of sausage (sure, sure), the dozen half-naked kids racing in and out of this burned tenement so amazingly detailed—They sure must have the budget all right. Look at this desola-

tion, all built then hammered back into pieces, ranging from body size down to powder (please order by Gauge Number), as that well-remembered fragrance Noon in Berlin, essence of human decay, is puffed on the set by a hand, lying big as a flabby horse up some alley, pumping its giant atomizer. (p. 374)

Besides being disconcerted by the shocking news, Slothrop may still be suffering the effects of Säure's hallucinogenic hospitality, but his sometime paramour, Margherita von Erdmann, whose experience of this kind of delusion is more or less continual, has no such excuses:

When Greta hears shots out in the increasingly distant streets, she will think of the sound stages of her early career, and will take the explosions as cue calls for the titanic sets of her dreams to be smoothly clogged with a thousand extras: meek, herded by rifle shots, ascending and descending, arranged into patterns that will suit the Director's ideas of the picturesque—a river of faces, make up yellow and white-lipped for the limitations of the film stock of the time, sweating yellow migrations taken over and over again, fleeing nothing, escaping nowhere. (p. 446).

Erdmann enjoys drawing others, like her daughter Bianca, or the American deserter Slothrop, into her fantasies. One of her "scenes" with Slothrop illustrates how discomposing her illusions can be under certain circumstances. Having been tortured and raped in a movie entitled *Alpdrücken* ("Nightmare"), she wheedles him into reenacting with her, on the original set, one of the movie's characteristically brutal moments. Slothrop's "role" was originally played by an actor named Max Schlepzig, whose name the deserter happens, at the moment, to be carrying on a forged pass given him by Säure. When the two realize that their playacting has this added, unexpected dimension, Erdmann's delusions are reinforced, and Slothrop is introduced to new refinements of his own incipient paranoia. The reader, meanwhile, is subtly disoriented. Neither Schlepzig nor Erdmann are real names, any more than "Grand Inquisitor" or "captive baroness" (their roles in *Alpdrücken*) are real identities.

And the "real" act—the sado-masochistic encounter of Slothrop and Erdmann—is merely an *imitation* of an unreal, illusory act—the sado-masochistic encounter of Schlepzig and Erdmann in *Alpdrücken*—though, as we shall see, the supposedly illusory movie has effects and consequences that lend it the most thoroughgoing claims to being real. Reality, in this episode, is layered. By peeling back the layers, one can reach a bottom layer, but it too, the acting of the movie, is illusion. Peeling *this* layer is useless; one cannot hope to find something more real beneath this final layer, for beneath it is only—the Void.

In view of this confusing of film and life, we should not be surprised when the headquarters of Vaslav Tchitcherine, a Soviet agent competing with Slothrop for information about the 00000 rocket, turns out to be a movie studio, or when our hero encounters Mickey Rooney in Potsdam, where the activities of the powerful seem more in keeping with a Hollywood premiere than with an international peace conference. Ironically, the characters who see World War II as a movie may be closer to the truth than those who see it in conventionally more sober terms. One can discover more justification for their way of seeing things by reflecting that war is an enterprise that often shares a vocabulary with the movies. "Action," for example, is a word common to both sound stages and battlefields. Both war gamers and filmmakers operate from a "scenario." Often one reads of directors who are "martinets" or "generals," or of movies that "bomb." Stars and combat riflemen have "supporting" casts and troops, respectively, and "shooting" may be done with a camera as well as with a gun. A "theatre," finally, may be either a place to watch movies or a geographical subdivision of a war. The phrase "it's all theatre," introduced on the first page of *Gravity's Rainbow*, is repeated over and over again (pp. 3, 267, 302, 326, 521, 722, etc.), as if to circumvent the reader's common sense the way television commercials do, by reiteration and unconscious suggestion. If the term "theatre" is extended to an enterprise in which one can get killed, along with thirty-five to sixty million others, then the distinctions between "acting" and "action," between war and the movies, between real and reel—are beginning, at least, to fade and blur. (...)

In *Gravity's Rainbow*, then, Pynchon imagines a cinema more substantial, more *vital*, than life itself; consequently, to return to an illustration we have considered before, Tyrone Slothrop and Margherita von Erdmann achieve only a wan approximation of the erotic and psychological power of *Alpdrücken* when they reenact that extraordinary film on its derelict set. The set itself, with its flimsy torture rack, its wooden chains, and its tin manacles, is an emblem of real life's shabbiness beside the existential richness of the cinema. Like the shadows on the wall of Plato's cave, movies are commonly regarded as mere flickering simulacra of the world of objective reality, but the movie theatre in which we find ourselves as we read *Gravity's Rainbow* differs from Plato's cave. We will not see anything more real when we go outside.

—David Cowart, "'Making the Unreal Reel': Film in *Gravity's Rainbow*." *Thomas Pynchon: The Art of Allusion*, (Carbondale: Southern Illinois UP, 1980): 31–32, 33–35, 60–62.

John Hamill on the Role of Sadomasochism

[John Hamill teaches at the Victoria University of Wellington in New Zealand. In this essay, Hamill argues that for several characters in the novel sadomasochism represents a failed rebellion against order and "the system."]

The "last acquisition of '68," writes Baudrillard, is a "move from political to 'libidinal' economy," based on the notion of drive (20). In saying that, he attests to the influence of psychoanalysis on the radical politics of the sixties. That politics, according to Baudrillard, moves from the view that sees society repressing sex for the sake of "work" to a view that understands power itself to define, demarcate, and distribute sexuality. Desire moves from being opposed to power to being equated with power, leaving room for the development of the concepts of the phallocentric and symbolic orders that relate psychological drive to the structures of social oppression. As general as that claim may be, it reflects means by which we can contextualize Pynchon as a participant in the sixties, whose historical revisionism addresses the question of the ethical consequences of the notion of the libidinal economy within a culture saturated with death. As a result, sadomasochism becomes a major expression of that libidinal economy and is dealt with in a variety of ways in *Gravity's Rainbow* as a crucial part of the heteroglossia that is an obvious and much noted feature of the novel. For characters such as Pökler and General Pudding, sadomasochism represents form of retreat into the self, a process of interiorization leading to the pathos of social entrapment. The novel examines the relationship between sexuality and power by dramatizing in microcosm particular power relationships in a sexualized context. If sadomasochism is a rebellion, it is almost always a private rebellion, a withdrawal into the sphere of private fantasy leaving the character open to the tyranny of a wider social agency. Characters are only ever, if at all, half aware of Them or the System in which they are enmeshed because the nature of their positions as technocrats and because of their ability to see tyranny and social power merely as signs of their private erotic fantasies. (...)

The moment sadomasochism ceases to be a retreat inward in *Gravity's Rainbow*, it seems to become a surreal hallucination, a ghostly image of fascist bondage haunting the Zone. That is manifest in the miniature "State" that Thanatz discovers in the zone made up of "175's—homosexual prison-camp inmates" (*GR* 665) from Dora, who have been released and have set up an all-male community in the Zone. That society, rather than representing a form of liberation from fascist oppression, re-enacts fascist oppression as erotic fantasy. Fascist imprisonment as the mediating image entraps those caught up in this triangulation of metaphysical desire. There is now no fascist State to "wither away," only a sense of home sickness for the bondage of the past: "Their 'liberation' was a banishment" (*GR* 665). The distance between pathos and comedy here is very slim. Metaphysical desire involves a nostalgic looking back to a fantasy of the past. The mediating fantasy, however, echoes too strongly the injury resonant in the idea of Dora and fails to provide insulation against the external world. Rather it exists as a tormenting phantasm in a fragmented zone. That is reflected in the way Blicero as "Schutzhäftlingführer" becomes more and more a mythical figure toward the end of the novel.

The themes of the desire for transcendence, paranoid interiority, and the preterite flight from determinate fate are reconfigured in the form of sadomasochistic desire in *Gravity's Rainbow*. That occurs on a dialogical level through the interaction of the individual character, given a framework of desire through the notion of metaphysical triangulation, and semiotic systems. That method is given instability, fluidity, and movement through Pynchon's insights into the treacherousness of the semiotic order that mediates desire; but for the individual characters, temporary and local stability is created by a continuing belief in the existence of the object of desire beyond the confusion of mediating semiotic orders. Heterogeneity is, paradoxically, created out of a multiplicity of monologically oriented discourses, each symptomatic of a continuing diaspora that leads from the modern to the postmodern.

—John Hamill, "Looking Back on Sodom: Sixties Sadomasochism in *Gravity's Rainbow*." *Critique: Studies in Contemporary Fiction* 41, no. 1 (1999): 53, 68–69.

JEFFREY S. BAKER ON THE RADICAL CRITIQUE OF AMERICAN IMPERIALISM IN THE 1960S

[Jeffrey S. Baker teaches at Moorpark College in California. He has published essays in *Pynchon Notes*, *Studies in the Novel*, and the *Review of Contemporary Fiction*, and in *Pynchon and* Mason & Dixon. Here, Baker suggests that *Gravity's Rainbow* describes a pragmatic approach to contending with the reactionary politics of America in the sixties.]

Across Pynchon's body of writing, there is an abiding concern with the radical democratic politics of 1960s America. That concern manifested itself as early as "Entropy," Pynchon's self-professed "Beat story" (*Slow Learner* 14), in which the reader is left, finally, with two distinct and contradictory images: On the one hand, we see Callisto's ineffectual paralysis, as he holds the dead bird and stares at the window that Aubade has just shattered; on the other hand, we see the image of Meatball Mulligan attempting to "try and keep his lease-breaking party from deteriorating into total chaos" by giving wine to the sailors, separating the *morra* players, introducing the fat government girl to Sandor Rojas, helping the girl in the shower to dry off and go to bed, and calling a repairman to fix the refrigerator (97). As Tony Tanner recognized, Pynchon's story provides a metaphor for a classic epistemological dichotomy as old as Plato and the Sophists. Tanner writes:

> In that composite image of the pragmatic man [Meatball] actively doing what he can with the specific scene, and the theorizing man [Callisto] passively attempting to formulate the cosmic process, Pynchon offers us a shorthand picture of the human alternatives of working inside the noisy chaos to mitigate it or stand outside, constructing patterns to account for it. Man is just such a two-storied house of consciousness, and in the configuration of that shattered window and Callisto's paralysis, Pynchon suggests the peril of all pattern-making. (18–19)

Tanner's analysis points up a radically pragmatic political agenda for social change (as reflected in the Beats' anarchic rhetoric), as well as a pragmatic suspicion of the theoretical and an affirmation of the experiential or particular. Both of those impulses embody a radically democratizing Emersonian politics that characterizes nearly all of Pynchon's major writing. The Beats' criticism of "Moloch" eventually gave way to the hippies' indictment of both "the system" as represented by the American government and an American middle class status quo. Similarly, Pynchon's writing has progressed from the relatively mild accusation in "Entropy" of Callisto-like American complacency to a more radical indictment of such countercultural concerns as two separate and unequal "Americas," revealed in *The Crying of*

Lot 49 by means of Oedipa's odyssey through the labyrinthine W.A.S.T.E. system.

In *Gravity's Rainbow*, Pynchon echoes an escalating countercultural critique of the Establishment's repression at home and murderous imperialism abroad. That work reveals the pragmatist's idealist tradition as a European "death-structure" identified with Nazi imperialism and "planned society"—a formulation that Pynchon clearly connects with America's Cold War rhetoric and war economy in the Vietnam era. Finally, in *Vineland*, Pynchon's radical impulse is reduced to an almost wistful recollection of the radical and anarchic mentality of the 1960s. That book portrays a Reagan-era fascism not only accepted but embraced by the American middle class. It points up that 20 years later society demonstrated the limited success of 1960s radicalism.

Pynchon, then, is a writer of and about the 1960s; and most of his writing, from "Entropy" to *Vineland*, is caught up in the egalitarian and democratic ideals of the radical countercultural movement. Eric Meyer has written that, on rereading *Gravity's Rainbow* today, with the benefit of critical distance, "it is possible to see [...] how much it is a product of its particular historical situation." For Meyer, the novel is "a text of 'The 60's,'" not only because it is "*about* that now mythic period," but also because its many themes reflect the same "anxieties of an America at War both at home and abroad" as prevailed during that troubled period in American history (81). Across his body of writing, Pynchon has advocated turning away from recognized authority and affirming a democratization of power based on the individual's intrinsic worth, the same ideas that drove 1960s coalitions such as Students for a Democratic Society (SDS). Philosophically, SDS based much of its politics and ideology on the pragmatic writings of C. Wright Mills, William James, John Dewey, and Ralph Waldo Emerson. Although few scholars have attempted to trace the influence of Dewey and the pragmatists on 1960s radicals in the United States, there is no question that the pragmatists had great influence on the radicals' "revolution." Tom Hayden, one of the founders of SDS, had written his master's thesis on Mills, and the influence of the pragmatic strain of American thought on the first SDS manifesto, the "Port Huron Statement," is clear. As Stewart Burns has recognized, protopragmatist Emerson, pragmatist Dewey, and Dewey's pupil Mills were seminal influences on the democratically based old guard of SDS, whose early manifesto became a rallying point of radical democracy for a generation of demonstrators and activists (57).

Similarly, as most critics who have addressed the issue agree, Pynchon's writing aims toward a kind of "activism." Edward Mendelson has written, "*Gravity's Rainbow* is a book which hopes to be active in the world, not a detached observer of it. It warns and exhorts in matters ranging from the ways in which the book itself will be read, to the way in which the whole surrounding culture operates" (10). Mendelson's notion that "Pynchon's book tries to fulfill a public function" (5) is reiterated by Craig Hansen Werner's insistence that "Pynchon forces the resolution [of conceptual] modes off the page and into our lives, where it belongs" (191). Similarly, Marcus Smith and Kachig Tololyan insist that "It is the extraordinary ambition of *GR* to help its readers toward [...] freedom" (152), and J. S. Hans writes that the goal of Pynchon's novel is "to get us so actively involved in the view that we cannot escape the recognition that it is our world, the one in which we fully participate, and the one for which we share full responsibility" (278). Mendelson's point that the text of *Gravity's Rainbow* means to be active highlights one of the many convergences between Pynchon's politicized aesthetic and the emphasis of the 1960s radicals on active political involvement. Like Meatball attempting to work within the chaos that surrounds him, both the pragmatists and 1960s radicals favored action within the tangled, muddy, and complex world over the platonic theorizing that characterizes Callisto's *modus operandis*. Thus the "activity" that Mendelson attributes to Pynchon's novel is in keeping with an American pragmatism in which the aesthetic, situated as it is within culture as well as human activity and experience, is always political; art is always either reinforcing or challenging (as do "Entropy" and *Gravity's Rainbow*) the cultural values and practices that help produce it.

Because much of the radical Left in the United States during the 1960s relied on the writings of American pragmatists for its democratically oriented ideological underpinnings, it seems appropriate to base any reconstruction of that radical critique in Pynchon's work at least partially on the work of those pragmatists. In examining their "idealist tradition" (from Blicero's romantic quest ideology through Dewey's critique of Nazi idealism during World War II), I place Blicero's obsession with his "Destiny" and the Nazi affinity for destiny, as expressed in the imperialistic notions of *Weltpolitik* and *Lebensraum*, in the same context. Looking at the analogies that the 1960s radicals made between American imperialism and brutality at home and abroad and the German Reich's earlier imperialism and brutality through Dewey's critique of German idealism, helps to place Pynchon's novel in the context of that time and that ideology. (...)

The ideological motivation for German imperialism in World War II differed significantly from the American decision to participate in that debacle and to defeat Hitler's National Socialism. Nonetheless, Pynchon would have us recognize that the United States of the Vietnam era, through a historical process in which big business and government cooperated in the creation of the most powerful war-based economy that the world has ever seen, is not so far removed in either structure or intent from Hitler's imperialistic Nazi Germany. The same "planned society" that the Nazis coordinated, based on Walter Rathenau's World War I German model, has been connected, in Pynchon's novel, with Roosevelt's New Deal policies and the business–government collusion that culminated in the development of the war-based economy of the Vietnam era. Moreover, the same "idealistic" tradition that fueled the Nazi war machine, in the form of a Nationalist consciousness that relied on folk myths and a supremacist rhetoric of hatred, can be seen in the American justification for the Vietnam War in the form of a Cold War ideology that insisted that the evil Communist threat of Red China threatened both "Democracy" and the Christian way of life and therefore had to be stopped before it spread like a cancer throughout the rest of the civilized world. However, in both cases, the idealist tradition that is employed to justify the actions of the imperial powers only masks a more materially oriented enterprise: for Germany, the mythic folk consciousness was used, finally, to cover a megalomaniacal imperial impulse toward global domination. In the United States, the high-flown rhetoric of the Cold War simply glossed over the material interests of a military-industrial complex whose war-based economy would benefit greatly from the war in Southeast Asia.[3]

Thus, in a most ghastly and unspeakable way (1960s radicals would have argued), the "ideals" of both Nazi Germany and Vietnam-era America were employed to rationalize and justify the inconceivable slaughter of millions of people in the name of "god and country." If the historical context of Pynchon's highly complex novel is to be comprehended, then his analogy between Hitler's Nazi Germany and Vietnam-era United States must be understood in the light of the comparison between these two imperialist nations that SDS and other antiwar radicals were making throughout the profoundly troubled late 1960s and early 1970s in the United States.

NOTE

3. In 1966 alone, the cost of the war reached $20 billion (Gitlin 301). There can be little doubt that much of the impetus for the Vietnam War was economic, particularly in light of the collusion between government and big business that characterizes our culture of late capitalism.

—Jeffrey S. Baker, "Amerikkka Über Alles: German Nationalism, American Imperialism, and the 1960s Antiwar Movement in *Gravity's Rainbow*." *Critique: Studies in Contemporary Fiction* 40, no. 4 (1999): 323–25, 339–340.

EDWARD MENDELSON ON ENCYCLOPEDIC NATURE

[Edward Mendelson is a Professor in the English Department at Columbia University. A specialist interested in 19th- and 20th-century literature and biographical criticism, his books include *Later Auden, Early Auden*; he also edited a volume of essays on Pynchon and wrote an introduction for a new edition of

Gravity's Rainbow. In this essay, Mendelson suggests that *Gravity's Rainbow* is not strictly speaking a novel, and it can only be fully appreciated and interpreted if viewed as part of the encyclopedic tradition in literature.]

In both its range and, one may predict, its cultural position, *Gravity's Rainbow*[1] recalls only a few books in the Western tradition. To refer to it as a novel is convenient, but to read it as a novel—as a narrative of individuals and their social and psychological relations—is to misconstrue it. Although the genre that now includes *Gravity's Rainbow* is demonstrably the most important single genre in Western literature of the Renaissance and after, it has never previously been identified. *Gravity's Rainbow* is an *encyclopedic narrative*, and its companions in this most exclusive of literary categories are Dante's *Commedia*, Rabelais's five books of Gargantua and Pantagruel, Cervantes's *Don Quixote*, Goethe's *Faust*, Melville's *Moby-Dick*, and Joyce's *Ulysses*. (...)

The political history of language in *Gravity's Rainbow* has antecedents in the accounts of statecraft that inform all encyclopedic narratives, whether explicitly as in Don Quixote's instructions for Sancho Panza's governorship, or by inversion as in the rules of the Abbey of Thélème or the decrees of the New Bloomusalem. Statecraft is a larger matter than social observation. Almost all novels, until recently at least, concern themselves not only with character but also with a descriptive account (in some cases prescriptive) of the specific society in which the characters live. Upon such description encyclopedic narrative superimposes a theory of social organization, normally a theory which offers itself implicitly for *use* outside the book. The writing of an encyclopedic narrative proves to be a political act, and the narrative itself tends sooner or later to be co-opted for political purposes—of which some, certainly, have been alien to the book's author. Dante's use of his native Tuscan in preference to international Latin had political consequences for Italian nationalism—or at least provided a focus for later political acts. In *Le Conflit des Interprétations*, Paul Ricoeur writes that the display of a world and the positioning of an ego are symmetrical and reciprocal. Encyclopedic narrative not only locates an ego, it also locates a culture or a nation.

Furthermore, the development of a nation's self-recognition, and its identification of an encyclopedic narrative or author as its central cultural monument, are also reciprocal processes. The idea of Italian or German nationality makes use of Dante or Goethe while at the same time canonizing them (in the original senses of the word). But encyclopedic narratives begin their history from a position *outside* the culture whose literary focus they become; they only gradually find a secure place in a national or critical order. Dante writes the *Commedia* in exile; Rabelais's books fall under the interdict of the Sorbonne, and their author has to go into hiding; Cervantes refers to *Don Quixote* as "just what might be begotten in a prison"; Goethe allows publication of Part II of *Faust* only after his death; *Moby-Dick* receives most of its early recognition in England; the last words printed in the encyclopedia of Dublin are "Trieste–Zürich–Paris." To an extent unknown among other works that have become cultural monuments, encyclopedic narratives begin their career *illegally*.

Short of committing a crime, there is little a modern writer in Western Europe or North America can do, as writer, to put himself in an illegal position. In any case, the illegality of encyclopedic narratives is never deliberately *sought* by their authors. The West's wide range of toleration leaves, paradoxically, only a narrow area for dissent—which Pynchon has managed to occupy. His elusive near-anonymity, which entirely predates his encyclopedic efforts, is a stance alien to our literary culture; and *Gravity's Rainbow*'s drastic violations of what remains of the tattered fabric of literary decorum assert a further distance from officialdom. Critics who praise Pynchon tend to gloss over the uncomfortable fact that he writes quite a few stomach-turning pages. Slothrop's nightmare of a descent through the sewers, Brigadier Pudding's coprophilia, Mexico and Bodine's verbal disruption of officialdom at the dinner table—or Mexico's urinary dissolution of the solemnity of an official meeting—are all gross violations of literary and social decorum. When critics blithely quote such passages, as if they were as innocuous as Longfellow, they do Pynchon a disservice in ignoring the uncomfortable fact that his language retains an unmistakable power to shock and disgust, without ever allowing itself to be dismissed as infantilism or mere noise. Only a false sophistication—or a terminally brutalized sensibility—can claim not to be repelled by many pages of *Gravity's Rainbow*. (...)

Yet *Gravity's Rainbow* is, in a profound sense, a book about endings as well as about charismatic origins. Like William Slothrop, going westward in Imperial style, the book moves westward, in the direction of endings, the direction of the tragic necessity of the *Abendland*'s decline. Slothrop's dream of Crutchfield the westwardman (67) resonates against the book's westward vision of the next war, whose first bomb explodes over the western city of Los Angeles. The final pages of the book rush forwards towards the west and towards endings, but, almost simultaneously, the book rushes backwards through time, and eastwards through space, to Abraham and Isaac and the Judaic origins of the civilization of the west. In the last pages of the book "we" sit in the Los Angeles theatre on which the rocket is about to fall—as it "reaches its last unmeasurable gap above the roof of this old theatre, the last delta-t." But the final ending is delayed: "there is time" to sing William Slothrop's forgotten hymn, now miraculously remembered, as the hymn itself recalls the "light that hath brought the Towers low," and all the Preterite of "our crippl'd Zone." And the hymn anticipates the ultimate cataclysm that has not arrived, the end of things in the parousia, when the transfigured world will bear "a face on ev'ry mountainside, / And a soul in ev'ry stone."

But the book only anticipates this last postponed transfiguration. For us, as readers, nothing has changed. The book's prediction of the eschaton is a metaphor of its own ending: for us, all that has been concluded is our reading of a book. The last delta-t is not crossed by fiction. The rocket falls *after* the book's last words, outside the book's world. And within that world, where all events exist simultaneously in written words now unaffected by time, we find evidence that we have survived the explosion. The book's first sentence reads, "A screaming comes across the sky." If we have heard the rocket, we are safe:

the sound that reaches us follows a destruction elsewhere. So, as readers, destruction has passed over us, and we have survived. But we have more of the knowledge that is required if we are to act freely outside the world of writing—in the world where acts have consequences, time is real, and our safety is far from certain.

NOTE

1. To keep this essay only unreasonably—rather than impossibly—long, I have assumed the reader has some familiarity with the book, and will need little exposition of events and characters. The parenthetical page references refer to both hardback and paperback Viking editions (the Bantam paperback references may be found by multiplying the number given by seven-sixths). With the permission of the editor of the *Yale Review* I have taken over a few phrases from my review of *Gravity's Rainbow* in the issue for Summer 1973.

—Edward Mendelson, "Gravity's Encyclopedia." *Mindful Pleasures: Essays On Thomas Pynchon*, edited by George Levine and David Leverenz, (Boston: Little, Brown and Company, 1976): 161, 171–173, 191–92.

GABRIELE SCHWAB ON CONFRONTATION WITH THE SPECTER OF THE UNSPEAKABLE

[Gabriele Schwab is Chancellor's Professor of English and Comparative Literature and Director of the Critical Theory Institute at the University of California at Irvine. She specializes in critical theory and twentieth century literature and culture. Her books include *Subjects Without Selves: Texts in Modern Fiction* and *The Mirror-and the Killer-Queen: Otherness in Literary Language*. Here, she analyzes the way the novel attempts to analyze the idea of rebirth and hope built on almost total destruction.]

The resistance of the Counterforce, to which Pynchon dedicated the last book of the novel, shows the pleasures of an ostentatiously staged and unbounded infantile regression mobilized against the fear of inevitable extermination. Rejecting both a fatal reality principle and compensatory mythologies, the Counterforce does not aim at a transcendence to pure being but at a "transcendence downward" into a world of farcical insignificance. Refusing to make sense of what should and cannot make sense, it hurls its sense-contaminations, its "non-sense" against a mythologizing semiotization of the war. At a "Gross Suckling Conference" the members of the Counterforce exhibit themselves as victimized children of a society that acts like a "great mother" who feeds, clothes, and finally devours them because what some still perceive as "systemic rationality" has gone mad and destructive.

The members of the Counterforce are the only characters in the novel who initiate a movement against annihilation. Significantly, it is itself ambivalent, limited in scope and unable to avoid the disasters of war. But just as significantly, it uses designifying strategies—that old weapon of the hopelessly inferior resistance—against an overwhelming mystified and horrifying reality.

One could venture to see *Gravity's Rainbow* itself as an "aesthetic counterforce," but the facile analogy grasps only some of the novel's aspects. The amalgamation of the most sophisticated art forms with the crudest ingredients of mass-cultural waste is certainly a post modern form of carnivalization that creates an aesthetic counterforce. And the infiltration of World War II scenarios with both archaic as well as contemporary mythologies functions like Bakhtin's reconstruction of an acting, accumulated memory. Inaccessible to a linear or chronological historical narrative, this memory needs to be expressed by a simultaneous fiction that functions just as do those Pynchonesque "interfaces," like a "zone of contact" (Bakhtin) between times and space.

The concept of history as simultaneous fiction is further supported by the skillfully interwoven theoretical intertexts. Heisenberg's quantum theory, and Derrida's critique of Western metaphysic are invoked to introduce Pynchon's hobbyhorse—entropy—the key concept that informs the narrative, structure, style, and implicit philosophy of *Gravity's Rainbow*. Pynchon suggests entropic processes may exist on every level of human experience, but he introduces a narrator who—not without self-irony—views and orders the entropic dissolutions from outside.

He does so by simulating a four-dimensional perspective which includes past, present, and future and which can clearly be seen as a negentropic force because it opens an otherwise closed system. Ironically however, this very perspective enforces the impression of entropy on the level of the experience of reading. For the reader will not spontaneously shift to a four-dimensional perspective but tends instead to remain, like the characters themselves, entangled in the linear development of plots. The strategy of multiple perspectives thus adds to the overwhelming complexity which is not easily reduced to an order. But the narrator repeatedly invites and enables a shift to a four-dimensional perspective, which requires an effort to go beyond internalized habits of perception. Thus Pynchon's aesthetic devices generate, in fact, a new type of reading. See from a four-dimensional perspective, the playful simulation of entropy challenges the reader's three-dimensional frame of mind. The internalized pattern of space, time, and causality that underlie our notions of history seem to dissolve into the contingencies of exuberantly growing stories. The experience of contingency, or entropy, can only be compensated for by a shift to a higher level of order.

The deliberately induced loss of orientation, and the strategies that help the reader to overcome it constructively, have a utopian dimension insofar as they anticipate aesthetically future developments in writing and thought that have also surfaced in theoretical speculations. The French archeologist André Leroi-Gourhan has advanced the idea of s transition to a four-dimensional thinking, later taken up in Derrida's *Grammatology*. According to Leroi-Gourhan, the technological developments in our so-called computer age will replace our linear, writing-centered thinking by multidimensional thought processes and practices that require a reactivation of preverbal, simultaneous, and associative modes of perception.

Thomas Pynchon was among the first to face this challenge in a novel which is nevertheless bound to writing and was written for "three-dimensional readers." Thus he contributes, in his own playful way, to leading us a step further into the differentiation of our own cyborglike subjectivity. Intertextual and intertemporal devices provide Pynchon with a literary form for a multidimensional concept of history and the self. These devices allow the reader to experience a different time-order and an ecological interdependency of historical phenomena *within* the two-dimensional framework of writing (*écriture*) and the linear order of print. If we want to make sense of *Gravity's Rainbow*, we have to learn to shift between these different orders.

The most radical implication of this new historical vision is perhaps the idea that the old "secular history" is a "diversionary tactic" (*GR*) which blinds us to the economics and technology of war. Pynchon seems to suggest that the transpersonal agencies assert their power through the channels of a traditional notion of history, and that we have to see beyond if we want to perceive and perhaps change "the persistence of structures favoring death" (*GR*).

This is where the new historical novel unfolds both an apocalyptic and an implicit utopian dimension. It suggests that apocalyptic myths of the Rocket or the cosmic bomb, as much as the actual occurrence of megadeath, pertain to a secular history staged by transpersonal agents as an "other scene" (I see an affinity here, on the level of a "political unconscious," to Freud's "other scene" of the dream). The dangerous ambiguity is that even this notion can be appropriated by strategies of denial that allow those involved in the war to reject their own responsibility. This is how one of the fascists tries to place himself beyond "History": "The mass nature of wartime death is useful in many ways. It serves as spectacle, as diversion from the real movements of the war. It provides raw material to be recorded into History as sequences of violence, battle after battle" (*GR*).

Gravity's Rainbow makes our dwelling in mystified "secular histories" as obsolete as the facile counterreaction implied in the notion that we are "beyond history." The text reveals that the "other scene" of history can also be that of the "political unconscious," hidden from secular history, which one can only reveal if history is read against the grain. One project of *Gravity's Rainbow* is to invite such a reading, and in this respect, too, it is an archeology more than a historiography. In the context of the two juxtaposed historical stages, the novel about the apocalyptic

Rocket turns into an "experimental" or a "second degree mythology" as defined by Roland Barthes, a mythology that demystifies because it is transplanted into a self-reflexive context. That is why *Gravity's Rainbow* is not an apocalyptic fiction, but an apocalyptic metafiction. And, as we are never to forget, it is a carnivalistic show subversive of its own totalizing tendencies. Its end is a "descent," a "final countdown" in San Francisco's Orpheus Theater, initiated by the audience's rhythmical chant "Come on! Start-the-show!" (*GR*). But the show is the silent fall of the apocalyptic Rocket on the imaginary world as stage whose end is to be invented by the reader. And yet: the end of *history* is beyond the end of *Gravity's Rainbow*.

> —Gabriele Schwab, "Creative Paranoia and Frost Patterns of White Words." *Thomas Pynchon's* Gravity's Rainbow, edited by Harold Bloom, (New York: Chelsea House, 1986): 108–110.

JOHN O. STARK ON THE DIFFICULTY FOR READERS PRESENTED BY SCIENTIFIC AND TECHNICAL INFORMATION

[John O. Stark taught at the University of Wisconsin—Extension. His books include *The Literature of Exhaustion: Borges, Nabokov, and Barth*, *The Almanac of British and American Literature*, and *Pynchon's Fictions: Thomas Pynchon and the Literature of Information*. In this chapter from his book on Pynchon, Stark shows how Pynchon presents science and technology both literally and figuratively in the novel.]

The scientific and technological information in Pynchon's books is responsible, to a large extent, for their obscurity. One can deal efficiently with it by proceeding in two stages. First, one can see how Pynchon uses individual bits of data. To do so, one of course must know what each of the bits means. Second, one can see how Pynchon adopts for his own purposes scientific means of organizing data. For example, he frequently refers to the Second Law of Thermodynamics, often called the principle of entropy.

Scientific laws synthesize because, as Stephen Toulmin shows, they "express the form of a regularity rather than merely expressing a piece of data or even a regularity." Pynchon also contrasts a cause-and-effect epistemology with a statistical epistemology. He refers often to cybernetics and mathematics, two synthesizing disciplines. The avowed purpose of cybernetics is to synthesize parts of other scientific disciplines. About the synthesizing capacity of mathematics Toulmin writes, "Complex sets of exact inferring-techniques as we have need of in physics can be, and tend to be, cast in a mathematical form" (p. 33).

Pynchon adapts to literary purposes both raw information and these means for synthesizing, using them to construct metaphors, develop characters and plots, and otherwise reconstitute in his distinctive way the elements of fiction that seem so chaotic when analyzed in the usual way. These unusual literary purposes and the unfamiliar scientific information in his work do cause obscurity, but despite this obscurity, Pynchon's use of information enriches his books.

Pynchon refers most often to scientific information that was discovered or became important during World War II and the information that resulted from that period's scientific developments. In fact, he implies that these developments may have influenced the course of history more than have the political and social changes that the war caused. Many others agree with his assessment. Arthur Porter, for example, claims that "all in all the impact of World War II military technology on the world of today has been extraordinary." Porter considers servomechanisms and computers to be examples of important technology developed during that era. In *Gravity's Rainbow* Pynchon implies this same point about the scientific advances of that time as he delineates the war's scientific background, especially developments that have played in important role postwar history. In contrast, although the political events of the war years are well known, Pynchon rarely emphasizes them. For example, his characters—scientists and nonscientists alike—react more often to scientific information than to political events. At the extreme, one of the characters considers the possibility that the war is no more than a huge scientific laboratory and that politicians and military leaders set policy so as to maximize scientific and technological progress. To elucidate this information one must begin with the rocket, the primary symbol and focal point of *Gravity's Rainbow*. In fact, nearly all the important scientific and technological information in Pynchon's novels and short stories focuses on either rocketry or fields that were advanced by efforts to improve rockets or to defend against them. Pynchon even sees sexual implications in the rocket; it is not accidental that in *Gravity's Rainbow* Slothrop's sexual relationships correlate with rocket landings. One character understands the rocket's sexuality thus: "Katje has understood the great airless arc as a clear allusion to certain secret lusts that drive the planet and herself ... toward a terminal orgasm" (p. 223). Throughout this novel Pynchon also develops the motif of the rocket's masculinity. Enzian, a Herero who joins the search for rocket 00000, learns that "the Rocket was an entire system *won*, away from the feminine darkness, held against the entropies of lovable but scatterbrained Mother Nature: that was the first thing he was obliged by Weissmann to learn, his first step toward citizenship in the Zone" (p. 324). Pynchon hints that Weissmann, the German rocket chief, has a homosexual attachment to Enzian and to the young boy who rides inside the rocket near the novel's end. Sexuality also paradoxically opposes the rocket and its meanings, for some of the people who work on it or search for it save themselves through sexual love from its total dominance.

The rocket also has implications for the philosophy of history that show another way to arrange information about it into a pattern. Nora Dodson-Truck begins to believe that she is gravity: "*I am Gravity. I am That against which the Rocket must struggle, to which the prehistoric wastes submit and are transmuted to the very substances of History*" (p. 639). In this view, history records battles against waste: inanimateness and other anti-human qualities. To extend this metaphor's implications, history is formed as each age rises above its predecessor. Nora, however, fails to mention the other half of a rocket's flight, the downward movement from the point where gravity begins to have more force than the effect of the initial impetus. If history is a rocket, it has a parabolic course, rising but then falling to a Spenglerian collapse or to an apocalypse. The war and the psychological and social conditions in *Gravity's Rainbow* support this belief that the world will soon collapse, and the novel ends as a rocket is about to destroy a movie theater in which the readers appear to be sitting.

During World War II, rocket programs hastened the development of plastics, as scientists synthesized new plastics or improved old ones to make parts for rockets and after the war used these plastics for nonmilitary purposes and applied the knowledge that they had gained in developing plastics to solve other problems. For example, scientists developed PMMA for cockpit covers, polyethylene for radar, and PTFE for atomic fission. Plastic as a material has also interested novelists because certain of its qualities have made it seem representative of our times. The simple, repeated chemical units that form the molecules make plastics a fitting analogy for a social structure composed of many simple, nearly identical persons. The molecules of one of the two types of plastics, the thermoplastics, are not chemically joined. One can draw analogies here with loose social bonds. The extreme moldability of plastics has been a major source of their usefulness, and again a social analogy is suggested. All of these phenomena, as well as plastic-like artificiality, are prominent in the society that Pynchon describes. His characters, often almost indistinguishable one from another, wander around forming unstable bonds with each other and falling victim to stronger forces that mold them at will.

By imagining the plastic Imipolex G Pynchon also adds his own meanings to this material. Jamf, the evil scientist who may have programmed Slothrop, invented Imipolex G, so it, too, is probably evil. Its development also shows the influence of international corporate cartels, since Jamf at the time of his discovery worked for IG Farben, and Shell later partially controlled the patent. To some people the history of Imipolex G therefore looks like a commercial plot. Plastics are aromatic chemicals, so Kekulé's dream of the benzene ring and all the associations that Pynchon draws from it attach themselves like carbon molecules to the motif of plastics. In this case, too, science has renounced its neutrality; the plastic synthesized for the rocket will serve the German war effort. Pynchon makes this military use appear inevitable by alluding to "Plasticity's virtuous triad of Strength, Stability and Whiteness (*Kraft, Standfestigkeit, Weisse*: how often these were taken for Nazi graffiti)" (p. 250). These first two qualities apply to stable plastics: the thermosets, which have strong molecular bonds. This statement almost makes plastic seem like a distinctively Nazi substance by comparing its physical properties to that society's ideals. Thus, going well beyond making obvious metaphors, he adds symbolic meanings to his work.

He also sees sexual meanings in plastic. For example, some of the orgiastic characters in *Gravity's Rainbow* dress a girl in Imipolex G. She admits afterward, "Nothing I ever wore, before or since, aroused me quite as much as Imipolex" (p. 488). More than two hundred pages later Pynchon explains why it excites her: "Imipolex G is the first plastic that is actually *erectile*. Under suitable stimuli, the chains grow cross-links, which stiffen the molecule and increase intermolecular attraction so that this Peculiar Polymer runs far outside the known phase diagrams, from limp rubbery amorphous to amazing perfect tessellation, hardness, brilliant transparency" (p. 699). In other words, if the girl dressed in plastic stimulated it sufficiently the plastic erected and they had a bizarre kind of intercourse. As an objective account of reality this statement does not convince, but as a comment on the sexuality of Pynchon's characters it does. Sex with a piece of plastic could not differ very much from the kind of virtually inanimate sex practiced by characters such as The Whole Sick Crew in *V.* (...)

Pynchon, then, is not a frustrated scientist merely leaving shards of scientific information strewn around in his novels, particularly in *Gravity's Rainbow*. He assembles these shards, impressive enough individually, into a vessel both beautiful and, because it orders and thus explains the world around it, useful. The glue he uses is a contrast made by Pascal, whose work exhibits a major tension between *l'esprit geometrique* and *l'esprit de finesse*. The geometrical spirit of the scientists and of the characters who think like them bears major responsibility for the war in *Gravity's Rainbow*. It also opposes a more dexterous and free-wheeling spirit embodied by a few characters and even more by Pynchon's own literary prestidigitations.

>   —John O. Stark. "Science and Technology." *Pynchon's Fictions: Thomas Pynchon and the Literature of Information*. (Athens: Ohio University Press, 1980): 45–49, 73.

PLOT SUMMARY OF
Mason & Dixon

Published in 1977, Pynchon's most recent novel, *Mason & Dixon* is in many ways a "typical" Pynchon novel: the jokes and puns, interest in conspiracies, playful language, and a framework in which narratives are nestled within other narratives which in turn are framed by other narratives, are all here. Like many other Pynchon novels, it is a very large book—773 pages long—and it is also nearly impossible to summarize, or even to tell, the plot of the book. But, once again, that "impossibility" is part and parcel of Pynchon's ongoing project in general: all narratives are "really" impossible, Pynchon seems to be arguing, and his books are "merely" proof of that that theorem.

As the novel opens, readers should notice the odd language, spelling, and typography of the text: "Snow-Balls have flown their Arcs, starr'd the Sides of Outbuildings, as of Cousins, carried Hats away in to the brisk Wind off Delaware..." Evidently, the voice of the novel is of colonial America rather than the modern and somewhat facetious voice of Pynchon's other novels. The second thing readers may observe is that it will take awhile to reach to the story of the historical characters of Charles Mason and Jeremiah Dixon, or their famous explorations and mapping of the border between Pennsylvania and Maryland—a mapping which later produces the well-known "Mason-Dixon Line," which itself plays such an important role as the country develops and heads towards its civil war, but which Cherrycoke himself describes as "meaningless."

It is 1786 in the Philadelphia house of Wade LeSpark, where LeSpark's brother-in-law, the Reverend Wicks Cherrycoke is telling a rambling story. In attendance are Cherrycoke's nephews, the twins Pitt and Pliny, and his niece, Tenebrae, as well as "what Friends old and young may find their way here, to gather for another Tale from their far travl'd Uncle." We learn that Cherrycoke in essence "pays" for his lodging at LeSpark's with these nightly tales. In fact, Cherrycoke is already bound up in a commerce of payment and yarn-spinning that precedes his storytelling at LeSpark's: Cherrycoke's father has paid him a yearly stipend to stay away from England because of his shady past. As a much younger man, he had posted unsigned fliers describing injustices done to the powerless by the powerful, naming many of the perpetrators. Convicted of the *crime* of Anonymity, Cherrycoke was at first sent to prison, where he learns his own name was never his own to give or withhold; rather it has always belonged to the Authorities. Cherrycoke as a result of his crime is styled insane by everyone, "so as to serve their interest."

Once these "interruptions" are over, Cherrycoke starts his story—which is quite often interrupted by his audience and their comings and goings as well as their falling asleep and waking up—with Mason and Dixon's commission by the British Royal Society to observe the Transit of Venus in South Africa. Mason, whose wife Rebekah is dead yet still in his mind, is disconnected from his sons and more sober and withdrawn than Dixon, while Dixon is more of a carouser, more attracted to wine, women and song—infatuated with attraction as it were. While in South Africa, the pair meet Fang, the "Learned English Dog," who is preternatural (that is, strange or out-of-the ordinary) but not supernatural—he describes himself to the surveyors as a kind of "tail-wagging Scheherazade." Mason and Dixon also meet the Vroom family, whose daughters are all nymphomaniacs. After their observations in Cape Town—both of the transit and the system of slavery in effect there—are concluded, and after a short separation, the two are again sent off across the globe, this time to America, to map the debated border between Pennsylvania and Maryland.

In pre-Revolutionary America, they visit "The All-Nations Coffee House," where each serving girl is dressed in the costume of one of the coffee-producing nations. They also meet quite by chance Benjamin Franklin, who is wearing the "tinted lenses of Spectacles of his own Invention, for moderating the Glare of the Sun"—sunglasses, in other words—and who alludes to numerous conflicts and conspiracies circulating throughout the colonies. Franklin also bestows upon them one of his pearls of wisdom— never pay retail—and tries to determine what political motivations may lie behind their task.

They also meet *Colonel* George Washington, although he is in a condition very different from that normally portrayed of our first president and hero of the Revolution. Washington, smoking the Indian Hemp he grows on his estate, veers back and forth between presenting himself as a rustic clodhopper and a sharp politico. While visiting Mt. Vernon, Washington's slave Gershom advises the pair on what to wear in the wilderness to avoid being killed by Indians and Presbyterians, and asks for their advice on investing the money he earns independently as an entertainer. Martha Washington also appears, bearing a tray of snacks to help them with their "munchies." At the end of their meeting, Washington warns them of the "Sino-Jesuit" connection and the "Army of Dark Engineers who could run the world" but who are being divided by an argument over Feng Shui.

Even before they begin their survey, though, doubt and uncertainty begin to creep in and affect them both. While Mason learns more about the "conspiracies" that are brewing across the colonies and of the "world that is to come," that is the founding of America as an independent nation, he is also informed of the pointlessness of his impending work: as one character has it, in the new America, "all boundaries shall be eras'd."

As the astronomers-turned-surveyors travel across the colonies, they take on an increasingly strange and even bizarre cast of characters. In addition to the younger Cherrycoke himself, the "crew" includes Professor Voam (whose electric eel serves as a compass), a French chef named Armand Allegre whose nemesis is Vaucanson's "Mechanickal Duck" (a robot fowl that no one can see), Stig, Squire Haligast, novelist Patrick O'Brian, Timothy Tox, Eliza, Captain Zhang, Zarpazo, a giant Gloucester cheese and others. Many of their "adventures" are anachronistic and rely on or mirror such current phenomena as cybernetics, the internet, and rock music, but this anachronism is also part of Pynchon's overall theme and purpose for the novel: he continually tries to show that our contemporary world's so-called innovations not only owe a debt to an older world and its technology, but also that the actual, physical connection between the distant centuries is much stronger and closer than we might otherwise imagine.

Even the background to this uncertain world the surveyors progress through is mysterious and perhaps unknowable. Mason and Dixon constantly encounter "beings" who can think and converse but who are normally inanimate: clocks talk to them, as do crocodiles and radishes. The stars themselves, which should provide the absolute level of stability and certainty for them—all surveys rely to one degree or another on a precision gleaned from the movement of the stars—nevertheless also contain mystery and perhaps judgement: throughout the novel strange sightings and beings appear in the heavens, perhaps UFOs and their alien pilots. And "underneath" the narrative as it were, exists the "hollow earth," a "complete, largely unsens'd World, held within our own," which at different times in the novel seems to "capture" both Mason and Dixon.

The surveyors glimpse that they are in all probability part of one of the vast conspiracies Franklin alluded to and that their task is much more insidious than the simple mapping and drawing of a line in the wilderness, a wilderness which itself seems to work against and nullify their own scientific knowledge and reliance on reason and logic. As one of them says, "To mark a right Line upon the Earth is to inflict ... a sword-slash, a long, perfect scar, impossible for any who live out here the year 'round to see as other than hateful Assault. How can it pass unanswer'd?" Once again, Pynchon uses the story itself to make this occurrence part of the narrative itself. Almost as soon as it begins, Cherrycoke's narrative is situated within another more anonymous narrative, and as it progresses is invaded by other accounts which relate facts and events—as the twins point out within the narrative—their Uncle Cherrycoke could not possibly know about.

An oddly matched and often antagonistic duo from the beginning, the pair ultimately become quite fond of each other, drawn together by their role in a project whose true nature remains uncertain and looming: in fact, at one point Dixon reminds Mason that they "must count on becoming old Geezers together." After their surveying work is done, the novel concludes in several different ways. In one possible conclusion, because "all History must converge to Opera in the Italian

Style," Mason and Dixon do not return home but continue exploring towards the west: "Suppose that Mason and Dixon and their Line cross Ohio after all and continue West by the customary ten-minute increments." As they advance, in this version, even though they discover America at its most enigmatic, untamed, and mysterious, a land overflowing with wildlife and awe-inspiring vistas of great beauty, a certain sameness obtains as well: another cast of characters, more "Difficulties" to be resolved.

But before the novel comes to final conclusion, we once again return to Cherrycoke and his audience. All the children finally asleep, only Cherrycoke and his brother-in-law, "the sultan," remaining awake, the "unchosen" of Philadelphia begin to come into the room: Black servants, poor Indians, Irish runaways, Chinese sailors, escapees from the madhouse. Bringing their scars, diseases, and unease, these dreams or ghosts invade the sleepers' dreams, but also instill something like pity or generosity in those awake.

Another more "realistic" ending shows the surveyors returning to England—after Dixon whips a slave trader on the docks of Baltimore. At home finally, Dixon continues his thoughtful if rowdy life until he dies of gout, while Mason attempts to build a more stable life, while at the same time describing the "Cometary Dazes" he is prone to in which strange objects appear in the sky growing continuously brighter as they approach—UFOs, perhaps—then vanish as quickly as they have come: "Do they watch us? Are they visits from the past, from an Age of Faith when Miracles still literally happen'd?" Finally, he has several new children with a new wife, reconciles with his estranged sons, and returns to America with his family.

"Already" framed by other, multiple and multiplying narratives and voices before it even begins, the novel ends in a combination of history, myth, and fiction—that is, in a fashion similar to both Cherrycoke's overall narrative and History "itself"—with Mason's boys arguing with him to be taken to America, where the stars are so close telescopes are unnecessary, where the Indians know magic, and where the fish jump out of the rivers and streams and into an angler's arms.

LIST OF CHARACTERS IN
Mason & Dixon

Armand Allègre, the youngest of four brothers, is an erratic chef Mason and Dixon encounter. He tells them about his fall from fame: once he was the most famous chef in Paris, but after agreeing to help a strange mechanical duck, he finds himself cast out to America.

Fender-Belly Bodine, a seaman on the ship Mason and Dixon sail towards the Transit of Venus, is one of Pig Bodine's ancestors. The pair encounter him again later in the novel at Fort George.

The primary, although unreliable, narrator of the novel, **Reverend Wicks Cherrycoke** is also a kind of Scheherazade who tells stories not to save his life but to ensure his lodging in the LeSpark home. A man possessed of good humor, a keen eye for detail, and mounds of information he could not have been privy to, Wicks also was one of the "crew" who accompanied Mason and Dixon during the survey.

Jeremiah Dixon is one of the two "main" characters in the novel. Scientist, astronomer, and surveyor, he is a Quaker who abhors slavery, but he is also dedicated to the pursuit of happiness and pleasure—in many if not all of its forms. Near the end of the novel, he beats a slave trader with his own whip before returning to England, where he later dies of gout.

Although an actual "figure" from history, in the novel **"Vaucanson's Mechanickal Duck"** is a robot duck who somehow comes to life, hectors Allegre and ruins his career.

Fang—or the Learned English Dog—is a "disheveled English Terrier, with a raffish Gleam in its eye," one of the central strange creatures in the book who add a magical or transcendent dimension to the rational or technical aspect of the unfolding survey. In a biting moment, the Learned Dog explains to Mason the true nature of "the dog": they act the way they do only so as to stave off for one day at least their own execution and consumption by their human masters.

Dr. Benjamin Franklin is the famous American writer, inventor, scientist, philosopher, and statesman. Though portrayed as a political plotter who attempts to set Mason and Dixon spying on each other, he also is identified as an American Prometheus who eventually attains great success in Europe.

The LeSpark Family is the main audience for Cherrycoke's narration. Presiding over the family is "the Sultan," John LeSpark, who allows Cherrycoke to reside in his home as long as he keeps the family—in particular the children—entertained with stories. He is married to Elizabeth or Zab, Cherrycoke's sister, and the father of Pitt, Pliny, and Tenebrae.

Reverend Dr. Nevil Maskelyne is the minister and Royal Astronomer of England. Historically one of the men involved in the "search" for longitude, in the novel he debriefs Mason before the surveyor publishes his report.

The second of the two "leads" in the novel, **Charles Mason** is the more sober and melancholy of the two. He is both literally and figuratively haunted by the "ghost" of his young wife, Rebekah, and is at odds with his children. Motivated by the need to escape this haunting as much as by his own curiosity, Mason, who "speaks in hurried and forc'd rhythms" eventually returns to America where he dies. While his second wife, Mary, and their children return to England, the two boys he had with Rebekah remain in America.

Professor Voam is a "Philosophical Operator" and one of the many curious characters Mason and Dixon become involved with during their survey of the Line.

Cornelius Vroom is the "pious" father of the Vroom clan, who Mason and Dixon encounter and stay with in South Africa. His three daughters, Jemima/Jet, Kezia/Greet, and Kerrenhappuch/Els—as well as his wife Johanna/Vrou—are all sexually attentive to Mason.

Before rising to the rank of general, winning glory as the hero of the Revolution, and serving as our first President, **Colonel George Washington** was a wealthy Virginia farmer and former surveyor. As much taller than Dixon as Dixon is taller than Mason, he is described in London as an incompetent fool. A "nominal" slave-owner who smokes quite a bit of the "Indian hemp" he grows on his estate as an "experiment," Washington is at once a crude bumpkin and a shrewd politician.

Father Zarpazo is the Spanish Jesuit from Quebec who "works mischief" south of the border—in the colonies, that is. A "master of disguise" intent on "controlling the very Stuff of History," he is the "Lord of the Zero" and is sworn to eradicating all heresies—especially ones that would cripple the Jesuits.

Captain/Doctor Zhang is the mortal enemy of Zarpazo. A master of Feng Shui who first tells Mason and Dixon about the "Wolf of Jesus," Zhang also supplies them with the curious "Chinese Tobacco." He makes a prophecy which is later ignored, that if the Line is completed, its only outcome will be "War and Devastation"—a reference, of course, to the Civil War. For some reason, the expected, climactic encounter between Zhang and his nemesis Zarpazo never quite comes about.

CRITICAL VIEWS ON
Mason & Dixon

Elizabeth Jane Wall Hinds on the Connections between the 18th and 20th Centuries

[Elizabeth Jane Wall Hinds is a Professor of English at the University of Northern Colorado. She is the author of *Private Property: Charles Brockden Brown's Gendered Economics of Virtue* and the author of several essays on Pynchon. Here, Hinds argues that in the novel Pynchon deploys extreme anachronism to cancel distinctions between the eighteenth and twentieth centuries.]

Mason & Dixon, via its lexical retrogression, temporal drift and class anxieties, deconstructs the eighteenth-century scientific project of mapping and dividing, among other gestures overlaying an eighteenth-century mechanical technology of telescopes and chronometers with a twentieth-century technology of satellite communication. Ending with at least two possible "futures" for Mason and Dixon after their New World adventure, the eighteenth-century love affair with strict chronology comes to a long, slow end in this novel. As Edgewise, tipsy, lectures his wife, "It goes back ... to the second Day of Creation, when 'G-d made the Firmament, and divided the Waters which were under the Firmament, from the Waters which were above the Firmament,'—thus the first Boundary Line. All else after that, in all History, is but Sub-Division," (361–62). The empirical, recorded throughout *Mason & Dixon*, so constantly generalized to the universal ("an unarguable approach to God"), becomes, however, divided by lived experience—a dividing line of human lives designed to cancel out the scientific equation.

Despite the time compression of its anachronisms, *Mason & Dixon* continually draws a sharp line between past and present, where in the past—language before the academies got hold of it, the calendar before reform—language savored of Nature. Even the silent slaves in their silence signify knowledge more "true"— more "natural"—than the scientizing Royal Society species of knowledge designed to rewrite the natural world. Language prior to the eighteenth century, Pynchon suggests, rather like Jonathan Swift, bore a closer relationship to thought and natural object than the list- and etymology-crazed pseudoscientific language as studied, as self-consciously written down. The pun and other wordplay bubble up out of the past, then, to challenge the falsely intellectual mapping urge strangling Mason and Dixon's compeers, just as time cannot, in *Mason & Dixon*, be trapped into a New Style in order to please the legislators; as in Mason's lonely eleven-day excursion, the Old Style, the ostensibly true round of days, will overcome the merely written, falsely authorized new calendar.

In this critique of scientific fixing of time and space, Pynchon draws a line of his own—between the Old, "true" and "natural," and the New, sterile, and intellectualized time–space matrix. A rather pastoral ideal, this boundary marker not for the first time dislocates Pynchon's characters, for whom the present is always the future, and so the past becomes if not idyllic at least understandable. Many of Pynchon's best readers have commented on his "nostalgia" or antinostalgia (Richard Poirier, Tony Tanner, Eva Karpinski, Maarten Van Delden), even in their disagreement acknowledging a recurrent division of the past from the present; at the same time, to use Joseph Francese's description of postmodernism to describe Pynchon's newest work, "the reinscription in the present of the detritus of history ... causes the recovered past to dialectically interact with the present" (6). With his anachronisms fleshing out *Mason & Dixon*'s temporal compressions, Pynchon thickens this dialectic of time by reversing causality: the present interacts with the past, too. Jameson describes this mobius strip of connection with a view of "Magritte's men in bowler hats slowly descending from the skies in the form of the raindrops that determined them to wear their bowler hats and carry their umbrellas in the first place" (185), illustrating a causality not linear, not reversed, but mutually constructive nevertheless. Such postmodern historicity does not preclude, however, a pastoral longing for a past seen, from one view, to be simpler and more natural than the present: "[E]ven the relatively postmodern revel in their own forms of the desire called the deep past," Jameson reminds us (175–76).

Not a simple desire for a return to a Golden Age, however. Pynchon does not represent historical time as the linear construct such a return would necessitate. I would suggest that history in *Mason & Dixon* develops as the theoretical parallel lines that eventually meet on the horizon, whereby at some point or points, "*everything is connected*" (*Gravity's Rainbow* 703), ever suggestive of the "caries and cabals" linking all events, past and present, in the paranoid's worldview (Tanner); for Mason and Dixon both, the "company" may well be directing every seemingly accidental happenstance of their mapping project—in this view history may well have a cause and an effect, however manipulated by the Royal Society or The British East India Company. History's other trajectory, running contemporaneously with its seamless counterpart, continuously removes the past from a present almost unbearably futuristic and unmanageable for Pynchon's characters. Charles Mason, then, stands facing the present in a rather Henry Adamsesque pose (an Adams infusing Pynchon's work since 1960 in "Entropy"), knowing the future—with its speed of change, its machinery-become-animate, with its "progress"—this future is here now: "[A]nd thus it happened," Adams would say of another and later historical moment of progress, "that, after ten years' pursuit, he found himself lying in the Gallery of Machines at the Great Exposition of 1900, his historical neck broken by the sudden irruption of forces totally new" (382). Mason, chameleonic representative of the fluid identity possible under the machinations of early market capitalism, breathes both temporal and historical movements—the rhizomic, interlocking webs of causality together with a linear history rushing forward at such speed that the future is almost past ever, as it is happening.

If, as Alec McHoul and David Wills argue, *Gravity's Rainbow* is "a book that is also a missile" (214), with its 1940s V2 a simulacrum of 1970s nuclear détente, with the ending like the missile always falling (or having fallen, from the first "screaming" that "comes across the sky" [3]), *Mason & Dixon* enacts historiography as whirlpool, fantastic as the Symmes' Hole (anachronistically, a nineteenth-century theory) reproduced in its later pages. Appearing in 1997, well after the fall of the Berlin Wall and well into a postnuclear ideological era, *Mason & Dixon* overlays a 1990s rather than *Gravity's Rainbow*'s 1970s sensibility onto its past. The web of history, it is true, bears a family resemblance to Pynchon's earlier work: the mysterious patterns or ghosts of patterns like global ripples from local stones appear in *Mason & Dixon* as in *The Crying of Lot 49*, constructing what Peter Cooper would describe as "an eerie feeling of *déjà vu*, a sense of some pattern revealing itself just beyond our conceptual horizons" (177).

Yet *Mason & Dixon* binds its historical period more tightly with the present of writing than even these earlier novels had done. With its webs of "real" Jesuit satellites alongside the socioeconomic web of Royal Society influence, not to mention the accidental webs of relations among lowly astronomer-surveyors and the likes of Ben Franklin and Thomas Jefferson—merely fellows well met in chance pubs—the "plot" of *Mason & Dixon* spreads rhizomically, literally to the farthest reaches of the globe. If traditional historiography "emplots" action in the past toward a hierarchically structured path to the future, in its plots defining the meaning of events as Hayden White characterizes it (9), *Mason & Dixon* deploys its several vortices of time-recurrent "lost" days and their cycles, anachronisms, returns to "natural" language—to disabuse us of such comforting eschatologies. Pynchon repositions the "detritus of history" not by moving his secondary characters toward a "primary" place at the end of causality, but rather by ensuring that no line leads seamlessly to the next—that all human action is literally and figuratively disoriented.

"In postmodernity," Francese warns, "primarily because of the revolution in information technology, commonsense conceptions of time and space are radically modified. The geographic mobility of capital to displace investments intensifies the demographic movability of industrial societies. The forced transience of the work force strips the individual of any sense of place or tradition, severely restricting the weight of the past in decision-making" (108). *Mason & Dixon* makes the argument that such disorientation in time and dislocation in space may well have been as much an eighteenth—as a twentieth-century phenomenon, in fact not only that postmodern culture existed, anachronistically, in a previous incarnation but also that the machinations and mechanization of early market capital—political, economic, and psychic—have come to result directly in the postmodern culture of increased disorientation.

Not unlike Oedipa Maas in *The Crying of Lot 49*, who looks at the lawyer Metzger with his perfect form and expects to see wires attached to him, so "unreal" is his body; and not unlike the V2 in *Gravity's Rainbow*, which brings the future right into the now since, once you hear it, it's already on you—like these characters in Pynchon's past. Mason, "middle aged" at 32, can never catch up with the future as long as his heart and mind reside in the past. Confronted with a rampaging future so near at hand, equipped only with a pastoral sensibility that casts a sepia glow over his own past with his beloved Rebecca, Mason, and perhaps Pynchon too, does his best to erase the lines drawn between the Old and the New, thereby erasing or at least effacing the New. Mapping of time, language, and space results, finally, in an erasure of the map, or the erasure of division between the Old and the New—to use Henry Adams's language to describe Emerson's mathematical approach to God, this mapping results in a "physics stark mad in metaphysics" (382).

> —Elizabeth Jane Wall Hinds, "Sari, Sorry, and the Vortex of History: Calendar Reform, Anachronism, and Language Change in *Mason & Dixon*." *American Literary History* 12, nos. 1–2 (2000): 206–209.

DAVID COWART ON THE CONFLICT BETWEEN RATIONALITY AND SPIRITUALITY

> [David Cowart is a Professor of English at the University of South Carolina. His books include *Literary Symbiosis: The Reconfigured Text in Twentieth-Century Writing*, *History and the Contemporary Novel*, *Arches and Light: The*

Fiction of John Gardner, and *Thomas Pynchon: The Art of Allusion*. In this essay, Cowart shows how *Mason & Dixon* both provides and relies on a semi-Luddite view of progress that seeks a balance between rationalism and mysticism—a typical feature of Pynchon's work.]

Early reviewers and critics, praising Thomas Pynchon for his confidence with scientific, technological, and mathematical subjects, may have overestimated his commitment to such material.[1] His allusions to *Scientific American* notwithstanding, the author's intentions seem always to have involved more than didactic exhortation of readers to become scientifically knowledgeable. He has suggested, to be sure, that humanists who ignore science can do little more than defer to—or rail against—the ascendancy of technologues. He has sought, too, to deny science the power that mystery tends to wield over ignorance. Yet beyond these arguments, in one novel after another, Pynchon has devoted his formidable powers of subversion and satire to exposing the false premises behind the technocratic syllogism. Thus in *V.* a woman seeks to transform herself into a machine. In *The Crying of Lot 49* a nutty inventor invites volunteers to communicate with Maxwell's demon. In *Gravity's Rainbow* various characters seek, as technological grail, the Rocket that will complete the abortive Armageddon of World War II. In *Vineland*, the villainous federal agent Brock Vond perishes in one of the "dead-black Huey slicks" he favors in his private, highly mechanized war against pot-growing former hippies like Zoyd Wheeler.[2] In *Mason & Dixon*, finally, an astronomer and a surveyor violate the American wilderness in the name of cutting-edge cartography. Here Pynchon scrutinizes the age in which technology began to come into its own—bringing with it the modern world's spiritual desperation. He exposes the fallacy of scientific rationalism at the moment of its great efflorescence in the eighteenth century.

If the seventeenth century saw an explosion of true science (Kepler's formulation of planetary orbits, Newton's optics and laws of motion, Boyle's chemistry, Leibniz's calculus), the eighteenth century saw science expanded and applied. Pure science (Buffon in zoology, Linnaeus in taxonomy, Priestley and Lavoisier in chemistry) vied with practical applications, as Watt patented the steam engine, Arkwright the spinning jenny, and Cartwright the power loom. Adam Smith demonstrated the logic of markets; astronomers strove to determine a practical method for determining longitude at sea. Diderot published the monumental *Encyclopédie* (focused less on philosophy and great ideas, one should recall, than on mechanical and technological processes), and Benjamin Franklin, that paragon of canny pragmatism, invented the lightning rod, bifocals, and a new stove while demonstrating the rational principles of economic success. Meanwhile faith in human perfectibility grew as philosophy sought, in human affairs, some equivalent to the laws of physics. Surely civilized humanity could return to the natural nobility still visible, as Rousseau suggested, among savages. Surely human institutions, studied carefully enough, could be made answerable to reason. The century reached its apogee, some would say, with realization of a great experiment in self-government founded on rational principles: the American nation.

In *Mason & Dixon* Pynchon anatomizes this nation on the eve of its founding. Like other novelists and historians, he identifies a strange mix of philosophical rationalism, spiritual yearning, and economic rapacity in the American salmagundi. But uniquely he settles on the surveying of the Mason–Dixon Line as symbol of and index to the forces that would become America. Like the kabbalists at the tavern called the Rabbi of Prague, he sees that the handiwork of Mason and Dixon may be read, in its cartographic westering, "much as a Line of Text upon a Page of the sacred Torah,—a Tellurian Scripture." As kabbalists seek mystical significance beneath surface meanings, so does Pynchon descry in the line arrowing its way into the continent a host of portentous intimations regarding the future of the nation whose birth, as the surveyors take their sightings, looms on the historical horizon.

Pynchon's views of the American eighteenth century incline, predictably, to the iconoclastic. Certainly the portraits here of George Washington or Benjamin Franklin bear little resemblance to the lovable figures depicted in older American histories. Franklin, his eyes hidden by spectacles that change color as often as the skin of a Vheissuvian spider monkey, represents mercantile forces that will elbow aside a host of spiritual and cultural alternatives in the New World. Washington, too, has his eye on emerging markets, and he dreams of an Ohio Company as rich as New York, Pennsylvania, or Massachusetts. The kabbalists may speak for the idea of a different America—now lost—when like Melville in *Israel Potter* they inveigh against "Projectors, Brokers of Capital, Insurancers, Peddlers upon the global Scale, Enterprisers and Quacks.... The coming Rebellion is theirs,—Franklin and that Lot,—and Heaven help the rest of us, if they prevail" (487–88).

Piety and weaponry. At once spiritual and materialistic, idealistic and brutal, America has always displayed the instinct for contradiction and paradox that Fitzgerald, an early literary hero of Pynchon's, probes with such subtlety and economy in *The Great Gatsby*. Pynchon, too, studies the American paradox, which shows to peculiar advantage, he suggests, in the years immediately preceding the Revolution. Subject to a fundamental duality, the United States seemed to exemplify the triumph of reason and faith in human potential, yet without sacrificing its identity as a place of spiritual distinction—a city on a hill. Indeed, Pynchon intimates that the Europeans who crossed the Atlantic in growing numbers were fleeing not religious coercion so much as the Old World's crescive secularism. America, to them, represented "one more hope in the realm of the Subjunctive, one more grasp at the last radiant whispers of the last bights of Robe-hem, billowing Æther-driven at the back of an ever-departing Deity" (543, cf. 480). Home to "the poor fragments of a Magic irreparably broken" (612), America was, absurdly, "this object of hope that Miracles might yet occur, that God might yet return to Human affairs, that all the wistful Fictions necessary to the childhood of a species might yet come true, ... a third Testament" (353, Pynchon's ellipsis). (...)

In *Mason & Dixon*, as in his previous novels and stories, Pynchon plays with myth making and the signifying loop, but not in any cynical spirit of iconoclasm. As a serious artist,

Pynchon strives to do full justice to the complexity of the world and history, language and the human mind. Thus he does not reject the possibility that spiritual realities have been obscured by centuries of what Derrida calls "logocentric metaphysics." One can argue, I think, the mounting evidence of Pynchon's spiritual and metaphysical (even religious) seriousness, his disinclination to privilege either the scientific and technological message or the endless lesson of textuality.

Which is not to say that Pynchon is, as the Hemingway character says, *croyant*. Pynchon insists only that undiluted rationalism makes impossible the apprehension of such spiritual reality as may exist. By the same token, though much exercised by the Line, Pynchon may not agree with those of his characters who construe it as irredeemably evil. He might differ, that is, with the reviewer who sees in *Mason & Dixon* "an indictment of private property, arguably man's most pernicious invention." Pynchon surely recognizes in the surveying of the Line a legitimate activity of human beings, who must pay attention to boundaries or lapse, as Frost hints, into vastly more primitive forms of territorialism. On this score one would err, I think, to take either the pronouncements of Zhang or even the late thoughts of Mason and Dixon as definitive formulations of authorial views. Pynchon's real attitude to his subject matter might best be characterized as Faulknerian: he reveals the built-in, programmed elements of tragedy in the human struggle with landscape and history. If he sees the seeds of tragedy in the totalizing assurance of Enlightenment discourse, Pynchon is not, in the end, the perfect Luddite. In the latter days of the rationalist dispensation he must make especially cogent the antirationalist case, but he does so less as mystic than as apologist for balance.

NOTES

1. Salutes to Pynchon's scientific acumen continue in the reviews of *Mason & Dixon*. Pynchon "loves the intellectual purities of science and understands them better than any American novelist ever," declares Paul Gray in "Drawing the Line," *Time*, 5 May 1997, 98. Pynchon is "a literary encoder of scientific arcana," according to Louis Menand, "a novelist with a message that requires,"

among other things, "an advanced knowledge of thermodynamics ... and the differential calculus" ("Entropology," *New York Review of Books*, 12 June 1997, 23).
   2. Thomas Pynchon, *Vineland* (New York: Little, Brown, 1990), 375.

> —David Cowart, "The Luddite Vision: *Mason & Dixon*." *American Literature: A Journal of Literary History, Criticism, and Bibliography* 71, no. 2 (1999): 341–43, 362–63.

Ashton Nichols on the Cultural Importance of Literary Epiphany

[Ashton Nichols is a Professor of English at Dickinson College. He is the author of *The Revolutionary "I": Wordsworth and the Politics of Self-Presentation* and *The Poetics of Epiphany: Nineteenth Century Origins of the Modern Literary Moment*. In this essay, Nichols suggests that in *Mason & Dixon* Pynchon uses multiple epiphanies to show how significant meaning can be contained in seemingly minor events.]

By drawing on the work of two very different contemporary writers, Thomas Pynchon and Seamus Heaney, I would like to suggest that the epiphanic mode pervades a wide range of literary styles, subject matters, and generic categories. Pynchon's work consistently reveals that words create fictional versions of experience even as they record cognitive elements of that same experience. From the search for "the direct, epileptic Word" in *The Crying of Lot 49* to the paeans to the astronomical "Transit of Venus" in *Mason & Dixon*, Pynchon suggests that moments of "revelation" are mental events linked to linguistic artifice, not metaphysical experiences of mystical transport. Heaney, in a related but importantly different way, appropriates and transforms Romantic epiphany into a modern literary form for the production of lyrical resonance and psychological energy. In many of Heaney's poems, the ordinary becomes extraordinary when described in a lyrical text that records a moment of heightened and self-reflexive cognitive awareness.

In this essay I will emphasize Heaney's most recent collection of poems, *The Spirit Level* (1996), and Pynchon's most recent novel, *Mason & Dixon* (1997). Both of these works suggest why literary epiphany is an interpretive category with particular significance for our own cultural moment. These texts also reveal an important way that contemporary authors use language to produce meaning: they present powerful verbal images that are never "explained"; instead, these epiphanic images are left to "speak" for themselves. In such instances, cognitive aspects of human experience are transformed, via literary language, into moments of resonance more significant for having occurred in a mind (brain) than for any precise "meaning" they might contain. Pynchon and Heaney offer verbal accounts of mental events that often *feel* as though they reveal "something" beyond the physical senses. But such feelings seem to arise only when the mind perceives itself in the act of cognition. The unstated "something" revealed in modern literary epiphanies is always connected to a powerful emotional awareness. If recent cognitive studies are correct, it is likely that secular literary "revelation" records the profoundly complex human mind–brain revealing itself to itself, and then to others, through the medium of language. (...)

Perhaps the most epiphanic passages in *Mason & Dixon* surround the Transit of Venus scene, that moment when the shadow of the planet Venus passes in front of the sun. Pynchon's imaginative reconstruction of this moment is, as so often in the novel, based on a precise historical circumstance, the actual Transit of 1761, but his language suggests a significant link between this most material of astronomical events and its cognitive effect on several observers. In fact, he uses the etymology of "epiphany" (the manifestation of a god or goddess, as in ancient Greece) in his first description of this solar and planetary event: "Thro' our whole gazing-lives, Venus has been a tiny Dot of Light, going through phases like the Moon, ever against the black face of Eternity. But on the day of this Transit, all shall suddenly reverse,—as she is caught, dark, embodied, solid, against the face of the Sun,—a Goddess descended from light to Matter" (92). Pynchon indicates the cognitive dimension of such a moment when he points to the arbitrary location of a pair of organic human eyeballs as the basis for such "revelation": "Remember to keep both eyes open, and there will be three Bodies, lined up perfectly,—the Heliocentric system in its true Mechanism" (93). Without the precise, but contingent, linking of three material objects (sun, Venus, human observer) this powerful moment would never occur. Such an experience could never be general or universal; it is the result of a pair of human eyes (and the brain behind them) lining up in an exact and specific way with two extraterrestrial bodies. The effect of such an intentional coincidence is startling. As the Transit begins:

> A sort of long black Filament yet connects her [Venus] to the Limb of the Sun, tho' she be moved well onto its Face, much like an Ink-Drop about to fall from the Quill of a forgetful scribbler, sidewise, of course—"Quick! Someone, secure the Time,—"
> ... the moment of first contact produces a collective brain-pang, as if for something lost and already unclaimable,—...—the Week of the Transit,—the Day,—the Hour,—the Minute, and at last 'tis, "Eh? Where am I?" (96–97)

All the terms of literary epiphany are lurking in this passage: powerful sensory awareness, brain-pang (cognitive event), emotional response, a sense of time stopped, uncertainty, powerful resonance over time, memory.

At the same moment, Jeremiah Dixon cries out. "Upon first making out the Planet, Dixon becomes as a Sinner converted, 'Eeh! God in his Glory!'" (98). But this attempt at turning a post-Enlightenment astronomical epiphany into a religious one is undercut when Mason reflects on the historical age both he and Dixon inhabit: "Isn't this suppos'd to be the Age of Reason? To believe in the cold light of this all-business world ... is to slip ... into the embrace of the Painted Italian Whore herself ... and the radiant Deity to go dim forever" (164). Mason's skepticism about the power of such moments is confirmed when he doubts even the efficacy of the Transit of Venus; of himself he says: "Foolishly seeking in the Alignment of Sun, Venus, and Earth, a moment redeem'd from the Impurity in which I must ever practice my Life ... your not-at-all-assur'd Moment of Purity.—Fool" (247).

Pynchon is even willing to admit that the longing for moments of significance in the face of modern instability is a function of a uniquely American sensibility: "As God has receded, as Deism has crept in to make the best of this progressive Absence, more and more do we witness extreme varieties of human character emergent.... Another American Illumination, another sworn moment,—and where in England are any Epiphanies, bright as these?" (358). In *Mason & Dixon*, the problem for Pynchon seems to be that wonder has gone out of our post-Enlightenment lives, either because we no longer believe in the transcendent sources of wonder, or because our varying belief systems (whatever they may be) are individualized and personal, always restrictive, always dumbed-down and flushed-out by the empirical force of our ever-more-mapped and surveyed, ever more controlled, and always-already-articulated world. The possibility of the epiphanic moment seems to hold out, even for Pynchon, the chance for a mind to make new meaning by way of a new combination of sensory event, emotional response, and words. (...)

In that regard, epiphany is a verbal embodiment of the way postmodernism reveals its romantic lineage. The postmodern mind feels significance even when it does not know what, precisely, is significant. The secular consciousness records its moments of powerful self-awareness and emotion even when those moments seem shifting, unstable and semantically unsure. As a result, postmodernist emphasis on language can produce a positive or a negative critique. The negative critique says that language is always arbitrary, that words can mean whatever we want them to mean, that we can say whatever we want to say. The positive critique links to a more naturalistic and evolutionary model that sees linguistic activity in terms of its success and "reproduction". Nancy Easterlin has recently argued for such an evolutionary model of literary activity that gets us beyond the political limitations of poststructuralist and materialist critiques of "realism". She suggests that "literary art" has "an ongoing adaptive and cognitive value. As individual readers and writers, we experience gradual and subtle expansions of perception and awareness that are indirectly advantageous in our dealings with reality".[10] Literary epiphany, as I have discussed the term, represents one category of such "gradual and subtle expansions of perception and awareness"; it offers a textual record (fictional, autobiographical, or both) of adaptive brain activity recorded in the mind of the possessor or perceiver of such activity.[11] Minds make meaning to help them adapt to their surroundings; successful mental adaptations (including language) then get reproduced and repeated as long as they prove useful for "survival".

This essay will have succeeded if it reminds us that minds are the products of brains (whether they are *merely* brains is a question I will leave to others) in human bodies, that language is a symbolic system that functions contingently but also with measurable forms of consistency, and that meaning is not so much a function of objective rules as it is a function of the growth of organic awareness and uniquely human forms of understanding. Literary epiphanies, in the unstable world of Pynchon's imaginative fancy (...)

reveal the power of the human mind to make sense of the material world by way of human language, a product of consciousness.

NOTES

10. Nancy Easterlin, "Play, Mutation, and Reality Acceptance", in *After Poststructuralism: Interdisciplinary and Literary Theory*, ed. Nancy Easterlin and Barbara Riebling, Evanston: IL, 1993, 120.

11. Recent discussions of literary epiphany that contribute to such an analysis include Martin Bidney, *Patterns of Epiphany: From Wordsworth to Tolstoy, Pater, and Barrett Browning*, Carbondale: IL, 1997; Sandra Humble Johnson, *The Space Between: Literary Epiphany in the Work of Annie Dillard*, Kent: OH, 1992; and Herbert F. Tucker, "Epiphany and Browning: Character Made Manifest", *PMLA*, CVII/5 (1992), 1208-21.

—Ashton Nichols, "Cognitive and Pragmatic Linguistic Moments: Literary Epiphany in Thomas Pynchon and Seamus Heaney." *Moments of Moment: Aspects of the Literary Epiphany*, edited by Wim Tigges (Amsterdam: Rodopi, 1999) 468–69, 475–77, 479–80.

WILLIAM LOGAN ON THE CONNECTIONS BETWEEN POETRY AND FICTION

[William Logan is a Professor of English at the University of Florida. He is the author of five books of poems: *Sad-faced Men*, *Difficulty*, *Sullen Weedy Lakes*, *Vain Empires*, and *Night Battle*. He has also written two books of essays and reviews on contemporary poetry, *All the Rage* and *Reputations of the Tongue*, and edited *Certain Solitudes*. Here, Logan argues that Pynchon's poetic tendencies in the novel ultimately work against its complete success.]

Poetry was the mother of fiction, and its reduction to a minor species of memoir has not been without cost. That poetry and fiction share more than they divide (fiction at times bearing the private burden of memory, poetry failing memoir in pure fictions) is often concealed by the hermit-crab isolation of contemporary novels, for which realism is old-time religion.

What makes Thomas Pynchon's *Mason & Dixon* a poetic act is not just its fanatic ignorance of current fashion (this historical novel almost makes a reader forget that beneath his cocky demeanor and hipster's cant Pynchon has always been a throwback), but its use of means, in its languors as well as its language, more properly poetic. There have always been fiction writers of poetic temperament: Joyce and Faulkner not surprisingly began as poets; minor poets, perhaps, but they took their early understandings of language through a form very different from fiction in its pretense, its rhythm, its design. In the last century Dickens, the novelist then closest to poetry, composed occasional verses as metrically right as they were poetically wrong. Though he has learned from the modernists by coming after them, Pynchon is a novelist of old-fashioned sentiments, not just in historical curiosity (his novels of contemporary life, *Vineland* and the thinly mannered *The Crying of Lot 49*, have been his weakest), but in his adoption of Dickensian comedy, beginning with his absurd and fantastic names.

The narrator of *Mason & Dixon* is Reverend Wicks Cherrycoke, a name Pynchon almost gets away with. One difference between Dickens and Pynchon is that Dickens usually gets away with his names—Dickens invents characters so true to their names they are false to their unreality; Pynchon loathes the idea of character, and his names wither into whimsy at the expense of character. The philosophy of names is too divisive to have bearing here; but there are few words more Falstaffian, considering the worlds they include, than *poem* or *novel*. Our unwillingness to deny anything with the ambition of being a poem the honor of the name may make discretion impossible, yet most readers have a Platonic sense of what a poem is and is not (that sense may be merely typographical). Though it may be modified by experience or experiment, this sense is unlikely ever to admit a doughnut, a desk lamp, or any literary act wearing the clothes of other conventions (whether diary, play, or novel, though there may be novels in verse, verse plays, and perhaps rhymed diaries—they may use poetry without being poems). What calls itself a poem may, within limits, be taken as poem; but those limits are less enclosing boundaries than liberated tyrannies.

Mason & Dixon is a novel, and yet the experience of reading it is at times purely poetic. Pynchon has embraced in his arguments and actions the crowded ambiguity and frothy imagery of poetry; and to examine them is not to suggest these means lie outside the novel, but to recall how long they have been estranged, not just from recent fiction, but from recent poetry as well.

> Snow-Balls have flown their Arcs, starr'd the Sides of Outbuildings, as of Cousins, carried Hats away into the brisk Wind off Delaware,—the Sleds are brought in and their Runners carefully dried and greased, shoes deposited in the back Hall, a stocking'd-foot Descent made upon the great Kitchen, in a purposeful Dither since Morning, punctuated by the ringing Lids of various Boilers and Stewing-Pots, fragrant with Pie-Spices, peel'd Fruits, Suet, heated Sugar,—the Children, having all upon the Fly, among rhythmic slaps of Batter and Spoon, coax'd and stolen what they might, proceed, as upon each afternoon all this snowy Advent, to a comfortable Room at the rear of the House, years since given over to their carefree Assaults.

This clamorous opening sentence, dense with the chaotic rush of new sensation (every novel plunges into the cold river of a New

World), is rife with the novel's animating themes—the ascents and descents of lives beneath those of the stars. Jeremiah Dixon is a journeyman surveyor, Charles Mason an assistant to the Astronomer Royal at Greenwich. The arcs and stars of those hurled snowballs are the heraldic signs of their professions: in the comedy of their lives, cutting arcs across oceans, siting stars, these characters make order from the anarchic motions the children in their hurtling suggest. The heated sugar is the earliest intimation of the trade that drove colonial expansion (its sweetness cost the lives of slaves): the lively microcosm (the whole novel might be said to be *upon the fly*, the characters ever in *purposeful dither*) serves a macrocosm yet unknown, a universe whose existence, whose author, is adumbrated by fond jokes—of punctuation called up by *punctuated*, of beginnings (and religious awakenings) summoned by *Advent*.

The microscope of the sentence reveals the universe of a novel. Pynchon is everywhere sensitive to what a sentence bears, eighteenth-century punctuation not taxing his inventions with the firmer syntax and fixed stops of a later era (the characters meet in 1761). The comic irritation of the capitals (no Bar to Readers of the Period, accustomed to such Emphases) removes the novel to the bewildering thicket of the past, as old-spelling does to *Hamlet*; but apart from its manipulation of reader psychology (we must become the readers of the past), the distancing of such capitals makes pastiche the comedy of form the way a sonnet is a comedy of emotion, the compression and entanglements of love finding their spirit in the spirit of form.

This intensity of imagery, this continual and immodest word-by-word invention, ruptures the plain understandings most fiction now requires. Novels must in part be linear and straightforward—they have somewhere to get to. Pynchon's have coiled upon themselves, devouring their bodies, as if distrustful of the long vista, cut straight through Appalachian forest and over mountains, that is the narrow goal of his novel's characters: the settlement of an eighty-year-old boundary dispute between Pennsylvania and Maryland by drawing an imaginary line, the line that would soon become the worried demarcation between states slave and free. (...)

If Pynchon's invention in language mimics the inventions of science, where one explosion is always fuse of the next, it is no more than the way science mimics poetry. The problem of this overstuffed work, what makes it finally a spoil heap of a novel, is just the poetic method that works so well in the microcosm. As exuberance and recklessness it is easy to take the petty irritations of Pynchon's mind—the bad jokes and worse puns, the cheap anachronistic references to contemporary phenomena. The pages are intercalated with songs and poems, but when Pynchon tries to write poetry, as opposed to embodying the methods of poetry, he shows a wooden and unschooled ear (even Jenkins' ear could write better verse). His heroic couplets couldn't have been written by even a bad poet of the period, having little acquaintance with the age's metrical practice, which would have been natural as breathing (even provincial poets could imitate Pope with success); but they're masterful compared to his music-hall frolics, like this Jesuit recruiting song:

> So,—
> Have,—
> A,—
> Nother look,—at the Army that
> Wrote the Book,—take the Path that you
> Should've took—and you'll be
> On your way!
> Get, up, and, wipe-off-that-chin,
> You can begin, to have a
> Whole new oth-er life,—
> Soldj'ring for Christ,
> Reas'nably priced,—
> And nobody's missing
> The Kids or th' Wife!

There is not a page of *Mason & Dixon* without its droll or disturbing invention, satires on colloquial speech (a milkmaid who uses "as" the way Valley girls use "like"), Jesuit coaches larger inside than out (a subtle slur on sophistry), a musical on the Black Hole of Calcutta, even a visit to the hollow Earth. Such lavish imagination (including his inventories—he's a lover of lists) has not been so magnificently sustained since Joyce. The novel's refusal to muster invention toward anything resembling plot, rather than just the spillage of events over time, seems finally a cowardice: by abusing the privileges of fiction (even picaresque's frivolous motions and meetings are a moral commentary on emptiness), Pynchon loses control of the advantages. His inability to exploit the contrived meetings with Franklin, Jefferson, or Washington, for example—he might have deepened his designs by ignoring their didactic promises—is everywhere repeated in encounters with minor characters. It seems not realism but carelessness (a carelessness so winning in the details). He exhausts so many small opportunities with a master's skill, it's a pity he has no interest in larger ones.

The novel's infinite deferrals, its postponed consummations (sex is on both Mason's and Dixon's minds, but every seduction is soured) finally become an aversion to any conflict or resolution. No one comes to grief; episodes both lethal and erotic collapse without consequence (a long-awaited confrontation between Captain Zhang, master of dark Chinese arts, and his Jesuit nemesis Father Zarpazo vanishes in thin air)—it's as if Pynchon loses interest. A novel may need neither plot nor character alone—Joyce and Proust offered character in lieu of plot and many novelists plot in lieu of character. It's difficult for a novel, even a novel everywhere touched by brilliance, to offer so little of either. Pynchon may have conceived *Mason & Dixon* as a supreme fiction, a poetic act freed of the slavery of plot and character; but conventions are cruel to those who betray them. As his stand-up comedy becomes merely a seven-hundred-page improvisation, the jokes grow hollow. Here Pynchon's poetics have seduced him: it hardly matters if most poems mean what they say. Poetry is the saying, but fiction (the drama, the action, the consequence, the regret) is the having said.

—William Logan, "Pynchon in the Poetic." *Southwest Review* 83, no. 4 (1998): 424–26, 435–37.

William McCarron on the Theme of Separation and Linkage

[William McCarron is a Professor of Literature and Languages at Texas A&M—Commerce. Here he contends that one of the major themes of the novel—and in much of Pynchon's work in general—is that separation and linkage are neither separate nor opposite concepts but rather intertwined and connected: different aspects of the same greater process.]

Pynchon's *Mason & Dixon* (NY: Holt, 1997) gives rise to the theme of separation & linkage before a word of the actual text is read. The title itself links two eighteenth-century men, George Mason and Jeremiah Dixon, whose famous Mason–Dixon Line would eventually become the demarcation between America's North and South a century later. Also, the novel's dedication reads *For Melanie, and for Jackson*, who are not two separate people, but one person: Melanie Jackson has been Pynchon's literary agent for a number of years. This article briefly shows how the separation & linkage theme pervades the novel.

First, in terms of the protagonists, George Mason is a Londoner, astronomer, and Anglican; Jeremiah Dixon is a rural dweller, surveyor, and Quaker. Even though these two characters will be linked in their journeys, first to southern Africa then to America, they are really representative of the two separate sides of the line they will demarcate across southern Pennsylvania; Pennsylvania is colonized by Quakers and Maryland is Catholic, though both colonies have Anglicans scattered among their populaces. In terms of the characterization Pynchon presents, Mason is introverted and "Gothickally depressive," whereas Dixon is an extrovert and "Westeringly manic" (680).

Herein lies a second extension of separation & linkage: the novel's constant contrast of the pre-Romantic and Gothic with the oft-mentioned eighteenth-century Age of Reason. With regard to the latter concept, Mason & Dixon adhere to rigid rules of star-gazing, line drawing, measuring, calculating, and note-taking as Pynchon delineates eighteenth-century surveying and astronomy in excruciating detail. On the other hand, the novel is peppered with continual Gothic—even anachronistic—motifs of separation: early in the novel, Mason & Dixon encounter a talking canine named Learned English Dog who "blinks" and "shivers" like L.E.D. (22). Certainly, Pynchon is here poking fun at a dog who transcends time because his acronym suggests *Light Emitting Diode*. Other motifs linked to the Age of Reason, yet separate from reasonable explanation, are Mason & Dixon's encounters with Vaucanson's mechanical duck which defecates as it flies at incredible speeds and a five-foot-long electric eel which performs in nightly light shows.

In regard to geography, the two scientists leave England and Greenwich meantime to travel to distant Capetown where, even in mid-eighteenth century, the English & Dutch are living together but constantly at odds with each other. Pynchon, surely, wants the reader to be proleptic and to link the early twentieth century and the Boer War which will break out between these two colonizing European nations. Likewise, any reader knows that the separatist Mason–Dixon Line will become the barricade separating the Union from the Confederacy with the key battle of Gettysburg to be fought in 1863 on the very cusp of Mason & Dixon's famous line.

The novel's principle scientific enterprise is astronomy where separation & linkage depend on the predilection of the observer. Each star is a separate entity, but men link the stars in constellations such as Castor & Pollux, Gemini, etc. In fact, the impetus of Mason & Dixon's journey to southern Africa is the Royal Society's desire for the two to observe and calculate the transit of Venus across the face of the sun—the coalescence, so to speak, of the orbiter and the orbitee, two celestial bodies which are linked but separate from each other.

In terms of historical figures, the reader catches glimpses of personages who are, in usual historical renderings, depicted as personifications of the Age of Reason; however, Pynchon chooses to show us their Gothic sides. For example, England's Chief Astronomer, Maskelyne, measures precisely, but becomes paranoid and unpredictable while stationed on the island of St. Helena. George Washington, soon-to-be father of his country, gets depicted as a hemp-smoking, punch-drinking fop. Benjamin Franklin is conducting electrical experiments with reckless abandon while nuzzling women and going on drinking binges.

Finally, occasional individual characters or events in *Mason & Dixon* are chiasmi which are linked to *Gravity's Rainbow*, Pynchon's 1973 novel set during World War II. To cite but a few, the narrator of *Mason & Dixon*, Wicks Cherrycoke, has a descendant walk-on character, Ronald Cherrycoke, in *Gravity's Rainbow*. So-called "Fender-Belly Bodine, Captain of the Foretop" (21) is the appellative ancestor of Seaman Bodine in *GR*. The mathematical joke of "What is the Integral of One over (Book) d (Book)?" (19) [Answer: log book + c, or sea logbook] is a forerunner of the similar log cabin + c = houseboat joke in *GR* (450). Obviously, the crossovers between the two novels are a kind of what-came-first-chicken-or-egg joke on Pynchon's part because *Gravity's Rainbow* pre-dates *Mason & Dixon* by 24 years.

—William McCarron, "Separation and Linkage in Pynchon's *Mason & Dixon*." *Notes on Contemporary Literature* 28, no. 1 (1998): 12–14.

Alessia Ricciardi on Experimental Postmodernity

[Alessia Ricciardi is an Assistant Professor in the Department of French and Italian at Northwestern University. She is the author of *The Ends of Mourning: Psychoanalysis, Literature, Film*, forthcoming from Stanford University Press in 2003, as well as articles on Pynchon, Fellini, and Calvino. Here, Ricciardi shows—through a comparison with Calvino's *Invisible Cities*—how in *Mason & Dixon* Pynchon reaches further and deeper into postmodern literary exploration and experimentation.]

A comparative reading of Calvino's *Invisible Cities* and Pynchon's *Mason & Dixon* might align the two texts on opposite sides of a dialogue between two aesthetically and ethically distinct varieties of postmodern literature. As John Barth has pointed out with express regard to Calvino, any consideration of the literary postmodern must account for the historical dimensions of the work.[1] Written in 1972, Calvino's novel is often regarded by critics as situated squarely on the boundary between modernism and postmodernism. Whereas it may be true, as Barth suggests, that the "postmodern" Calvino can be seen as a more modern modernist, Pynchon, whose latest novel appears just a few years prior to the end of the millennium, clearly is embarked on a farther-ranging exploration of postmodern territory.[2] Any dialogue between the two works might well ground itself in this sense of the historical development of literary postmodernism, which too often is reduced, as Hegel said of Schelling's notion of the Absolute, to a night in which all cows are black. (...)

According to Sven Birkerts, Pynchon's work represents a "metaphysical picaresque" novel that wildly reimagines the real life story of Charles Mason and Jeremiah Dixon, the British surveyors and astronomers who, between 1765 and 1768, mapped out the boundary between Pennsylvania and Maryland, dividing the American colonies into North and South (Birkerts 6). This postmodern fiction deploys an eighteenth-century narrative frame introduced by the apocryphal voice of Pynchon's Reverend Cherrycoke, a companion of the two Surveyors in adventure. Mason and Dixon themselves represent comic opposites after the manner of Don Quixote and Sancho Panza, with Mason cast as the melancholic, Deist astronomer from Gloucestershire and Dixon as the instinctive, radical, populist, and more pragmatic land surveyor from Durham, a Quaker appalled by the cruelty of American life. What ensues is a dire confrontation between the Spirit of the Enlightenment and the lunatic reality of colonialism as brought to life by the imperious cruelty of European slave-traders. As this drama unfolds, Mason and Dixon encounter a dizzying array of figures both historical and apocryphal that includes George Washington, Thomas

Jefferson, Samuel Johnson and James Boswell, a feng-shui expert named Captain Zhang, a talking dog, the golem, and Vaucanson's mechanical duck, this last an irresistibly sly comment on "the Age, with its Faith in a Mechanickal Ingenuity" (449). America, as it is imagined in Pynchon's novel, appears to attract magnetically all kinds of fugitives and dreamers.

The basic narrative, then, looks like a failed quest romance insofar as the line drawn by the two surveyors is of little help in mapping the uncharted continent and thus creating order out of chaos. Finally, the characters will end up questioning the very principle of mapping, as the project of the line increasingly comes to symbolize the frontier's violence. It is precisely through its artificial formalization of the border between a free and a slave state that the line serves as a reminder of the pervasive ugliness of colonialism, constantly bringing to mind the white man's massacre of the Indians and the brutal commerce of slavery. Mason and Dixon cannot escape an awareness in the end that maps, knowledge, and power are perversely connected to one another. Pynchon's farcical "vaudeville" thus is permeated by the tragic understanding that cutting a line between a free and a slave state means to maintain the convenient illusion that slavery, as Dixon puts it, is "ever somewhere else," in South Africa or Maryland, perhaps, but "never in Holland, nor in England, that Garden of Fools" (692–93). (...)

The aspiration behind *Mason & Dixon* is precisely not to redeem reality through aesthetic or literary means, if such beautification should preclude the imagination from acts of witnessing, from the minimalist forms of political engagement appropriate to the end of the millennium. In light of this position, it is more than likely that Calvino would have considered Pynchon's work insufficiently resistant to the "mare dell'oggettività" responsible, according to the Italian author, for the growing sense of vacuity or vagueness infecting the literary enterprise (*Saggi* 1: 52–60). Throughout his career, Calvino remained highly critical of any "visceral" or beatnik strain of literature, a genealogy in which, at least to some extent, Pynchon's work may be inscribed and that Calvino felt was doomed to conflate subject and object without hope of aesthetic redemption (Ferretti 62–63). By the same token, it is difficult to picture Pynchon as wholeheartedly endorsing the values espoused by Calvino as his ideals for the next millennium with the sole, probable exception of multiplicity. Rather than lightness, quickness, exactitude, or visibility, more appropriate signifiers for Pynchon's writing might be "gravity" or, perhaps, "rupture." It is important, precisely with regard to this contrast between the two authors, to note that at least one recent critic has argued that the first three of Calvino's ideals are, at their core, modernist values and, as such, removed from the entropic sphere of postmodern literature and thought (Musarra-Schroeder 45).

Pynchon's imagination strives to belong to the infernal *koinè*, to a dystopian universe for which there can be no adequate aesthetic compensation, and yet in its fearless lingering we may recognize a valuable stance. We ought to keep in mind that Mason and Dixon are deeply altered by their globe-trotting experiences and, once back in England, refuse to perceive their native land in terms of recuperation and reappropriation, planning instead to set sail again for America. As Pynchon writes, "They are content to reside like Ferrymen or Bridge-keepers, ever in a Ubiquity of Flow, before a ceaseless Spectacle of Transition" (713). On this score, Mason and Dixon should be regarded as the true inheritors not only of the Heideggerian preoccupation with caring for the past, but also of the very Heideggerian human topography. In his late and enigmatic essay of 1952, "Building Dwelling Thinking," Heidegger establishes an equivalence between building and thinking as forms of dwelling, which is to say, forms of caring, of putting at peace, of "staying with things" (329). It is in this essay that Heidegger ascribes to the figure of the bridge the function of gathering the fourfold of the earth, sky, divinities, and mortals (331). As "Bridge-keepers" who are profoundly religious land surveyors and astronomers, Mason and Dixon provide a pair of the most authentic figures of poetic dwellers in contemporary literature. They achieve the poetic through their very effort to acknowledge and to gather whatever is left of their human experience, rather than to transcend it.

Notes

1. For Barth's classification of Calvino, see *Further Fridays* 298.
2. Unlike Hutcheon, Dombrowski, McHale, and most critics, Barth essentially regards *Invisible Cities* as a modernist text (*The Friday Book* 196).

> —Alessia Ricciardi, "Lightness and Gravity: Calvino, Pynchon, and Postmodernity." *MLN* 114, no. 5 (1999): 1062, 1065–66, 1071–72.

WORKS BY
Thomas Pynchon

"Mortality and Mercy in Vienna," 1959.

"Togetherness," 1960.

V., 1963.

"A Gift of Books," 1965.

The Crying of Lot 49, 1966.

"A Journey Into The Mind of Watts," 1966.

Gravity's Rainbow, 1973.

Slow Learner, 1984.

"Is It O.K. To Be A Luddite?," 1984.

Vineland, 1990.

"Nearer, My Couch, To Thee," 1993.

"Spiked! The Music of Spike Jones," 1994.

"Nobody's Cool," 1995.

Mason & Dixon, 1998.

WORKS ABOUT
Thomas Pynchon

Baker, Jeffrey S. "Amerikkka Über Alles: German Nationalism, American Imperialism, and The 1960s Antiwar Movement in *Gravity's Rainbow*." *Critique: Studies In Contemporary Fiction* 40, no. 4 (1999): 323–41.

Bérubé, Michael. *Marginal Forces/Cultural Centers: Tolson, Pynchon, and the Politics of the Canon*. Ithaca: Cornell University Press, 1992.

Berressem, Hanjo. "Criticism & Pynchon & *Mason & Dixon*." *Contemporary Literature* 42, no. 4 (2001): 834–41.

———. *Pynchon's Poetics: Interfacing Theory and Text*. Urbana: University of Illinois Press, 1993.

Bloom, Harold. *Thomas Pynchon: Modern Critical Views*. New York: Chelsea House, 1986.

Brown, Donald. "A Pynchon For The Nineties." *Poetics Today* 18, no. 1 (1997): 95–112.

Brownlie, Alan W. *Thomas Pynchon's Narratives: Subjectivity and Problems of Knowing*. New York: Peter Lang, 2000.

Caesar, Terry. "Picturing Pynchon." *Gettysburg Review* 12, no. 1 (1999): 87–93.

Clerc, Charles. *Approaches to* Gravity's Rainbow. Columbus: Ohio State University Press, 1983.

Cornis-Pope, Marcel. "Rethinking Postmodern Liminality: Marginocentric Characters and Projects in Thomas Pynchon's Polysystemic Fiction." *Symploke: A Journal For The Intermingling of Literary, Cultural and Theoretical Scholarship* 5, nos. 1–2 (1999): 27–47.

Cowart, David. "Pynchon and the Sixties." *Critique: Studies In Contemporary Fiction* 41, no. 1 (1999): 3–12.

———."The Luddite Vision: Mason & Dixon." *American Literature: A Journal of Literary History, Criticism, and Bibliography* 71, no. 2 (1999): 341–63.

———. *Thomas Pynchon: The Art of Allusion*. Carbondale: Southern Illinois University Press, 1980.

Dugdale, John. *Thomas Pynchon: Allusive Parables of Power*. New York: St. Martin's Press, 1990.

Eddins, Dwight. *The Gnostic Pynchon*. Bloomington: Indiana University Press, 1990.

Flaxman, Gregory. "Oedipa Crisis: Paranoia and Prohibition in *The Crying of Lot 49.*" *Pynchon Notes* 40–41, (1997): 41–60.

Grant, J. Kerry. *A Companion to V.* Athens: University of Georgia Press, 2001.

Hamill, John. "Looking Back on Sodom: Sixties Sadomasochism in *Gravity's Rainbow.*" *Critique: Studies in Contemporary Fiction* 41, no. 1 (1999): 53–70.

Hawthorne, Mark D. "A 'Hermaphrodite Sort of Deity': Sexuality, Gender, and Gender Blending in Thomas Pynchon's *V.*" *Studies in the Novel* 29, no. 1 (1997): 74–93.

Hipkiss, Robert A. *The American Absurd: Pynchon, Vonnegut, and Barth.* Port Washington, N.Y.: Associated Faculty Press, 1984.

Horvath, Brooke and Irving Malin. *Pynchon and Mason & Dixon.* Newark: University of Delaware Press, 2000. Ps3566.Y55 M37 2000

Hume, Kathryn. *Pynchon's Mythography: An Approach to* Gravity's Rainbow. Carbondale: Southern Illinois University Press, 1987.

Ivison, Douglas. "Outhouses of the European Soul: Imperialism in Thomas Pynchon." *Pynchon Notes* 40–41, (1997): 134–43.

Jasper, Alison T. "Thomas Pynchon's Absurd Truths: Puns and Metaphor in *The Crying of Lot 49.*" *Arkansas Review* 5, no. 1–2 (1996): 39–67.

Keesey, Douglas. "*Mason & Dixon* on the Line: A Reception Study." *Pynchon Notes* 36–39, (1995–1996): 165–78.

Kharpertian, Theodore D. *A Hand to Turn the Time: The Menippean Satires of Thomas Pynchon.* Rutherford: Fairleigh Dickinson University Press, 1990.

Kupsch, Kenneth. "Finding V." *Twentieth Century Literature: A Scholarly and Critical Journal* 44, no. 4 (1998): 428–46.

Levine, George and David Leverenz. *Mindful Pleasures: Essays on Thomas Pynchon.* Boston: Little, Brown, 1976.

Maus, Derek. "Kneeling Before the Fathers' Wand: Violence, Eroticism and Paternalism in Thomas Pynchon's *V.* and J.M. Coetzee's *Dusklands.*" *Journal of Literary Studies/Tydskrif Vir Literatuurwetenskap* 15, nos. 1–2 (1999): 195–217.

Mackey, Douglas A. *The Rainbow Quest of Thomas Pynchon.* San Bernardino: Borgo Press, 1980.

Madsen, Deborah L. *The Postmodernist Allegories of Thomas Pynchon.* New York: St. Martin's Press, 1991.

Maltby, Paul. *Dissident Postmodernists: Barthelme, Coover, Pynchon.* Philadelphia: University of Pennsylvania Press, 1991.

Mattessich, Stefan. "Ekphrasis, Escape, and Thomas Pynchon's *The Crying of Lot 49*." *Postmodern Culture: An Electronic Journal of Interdisciplinary Criticism* 8, no. 3 (1998): 24 Paragraphs.

McHugh, Patrick. "Cultural Politics, Postmodernism, and White Guys: Affect in *Gravity's Rainbow*." *College Literature* 28, no. 2 (2001): 1–28.

Mchoul, Alec and David Wills. *Writing Pynchon: Strategies in Fictional Analysis*. Urbana: University of Illinois Press, 1990.

Mckenna, Christopher J. "'A Kiss of Cosmic Pool Balls': Technological Paradigms and Narrative Expectations Collide in *The Crying of Lot 49*." *Cultural Critique* 44 (2000): 30–42.

Mendelson, Edward. *Pynchon: A Collection of Critical Essays*. Englewood Cliffs: Prentice-Hall, 1978.

Modoro, Dana. "The Scholar-Magicians of The Zone." *Studies In The Novel* 33, no. 3 (2001): 351–57.

———. "The Sieve and The Rainbow Serpent: Bleeding *Gravity's Rainbow*." *Journal of Narrative Technique* 28, No. 2 (1998): 186–213.

Moore, Thomas. *The Style of Connectedness*: Gravity's Rainbow *and Thomas Pynchon*. Columbia: University of Missouri, 1987.

Newman, Robert D. *Understanding Thomas Pynchon*. Columbia: University of South Carolina Press, 1986.

Neighbors, Jim. "Kant, Terror and Aporethics in *Gravity's Rainbow*." *Pynchon Notes* 42–43, (1998): 275–91.

Noya, José. "Mapping The 'Unmappable': Inhabiting the Fantastic Interface of *Gravity's Rainbow*." *Studies in the Novel* 29, no. 4 (1997): 512–37.

O'Donnell, Patrick. *New Essays on* The Crying of Lot 49. Cambridge: Cambridge University Press, 1991.

Patell, Cyrus R.K. *Negative Liberties: Morrison, Pynchon, and The Problem of Liberal Ideology*. Durham: Duke University Press, 2001.

Pearce, Richard. *Critical Essays on Thomas Pynchon*. Boston: G.K. Hall, 1981.

Plater, William M. *The Grim Phoenix: Reconstructing Thomas Pynchon*. Bloomington: Indiana University Press, 1978.

Price, Victoria H. *Christian Allusions in the Novels of Thomas Pynchon*. New York : P. Lang, 1989.

Safer, Elaine B. *The Contemporary American Comic Epic: The Novels of Barth, Pynchon, Gaddis, and Kesey*. Detroit: Wayne State University Press, 1988.

Schaub, Thomas. "The Environmental Pynchon: *Gravity's Rainbow* and the Ecological Context." *Pynchon Notes* 42–43, (1998): 59–72.

———. *Pynchon, The Voice of Ambiguity*. Urbana: University of Illinois Press, 1981.

Seed, David. *The Fictional Labyrinths of Thomas Pynchon*. Iowa City: University of Iowa Press, 1988.

Siegel, Mark Richard. *Pynchon: Creative Paranoia in* Gravity's Rainbow. Port Washington, N.Y.: Kennikat Press, 1978.

Stark, John O. *Pynchon's Fictions: Thomas Pynchon and the Literature of Information*. Athens: Ohio University Press, 1980.

Tanner, Tony. *Thomas Pynchon*. New York: Methuen, 1982.

Sanders, Mark. "The Politics of Literary Reinscription in Thomas Pynchon's *V.*": *Critique: Studies in Contemporary Fiction* 39, no. 1 (1997): 81–96.

Wood, Michael. "Pynchon's *Mason & Dixon*." *Raritan: A Quarterly Review* 17, no. 4 (1998): 120–30.

ACKNOWLEDGMENTS

"Maxwell's Demon, Entropy, Information: *The Crying of Lot 49*" by Anne Mangel. From *Mindful Pleasures: Essays On Thomas Pynchon* edited by George Levine and David Leverenz, (Boston: Little, Brown and Company, 1976): pp. 87–100. © 1976 by Anne Mangel. Reprinted by permission.

"The Use of Codes in *The Crying of Lot 49*" by Frank Kermode. From *Thomas Pynchon: Modern Critical Views* edited by Harold Bloom, (New York: Chelsea House Publishers, 1986): pp. 11–14. © 1986 by Chelsea House Publishers. Reprinted by permission.

"'A Metaphor of God Knew Many Parts': The Engine that Drives *The Crying of Lot 49*" by N. Katherine Hayles. From *New Essays on* The Crying of Lot 49, edited by Patrick O'Donnell (Cambridge: Cambridge UP, 1991): pp. 97–100, 121–122. © 1991 by Cambridge University Press. Reprinted with the permission of Cambridge University Press.

"Oedipa Crisis: Paranoia and Prohibition in *The Crying of Lot 49*" by Gregory Flaxman. From *Pynchon Notes* 40–41 (1997): pp. 41, 56–58. © 1997 by Gregory Flaxman. Reprinted by permission of the author.

"Comic Escape and Anti-Vision: *V.* and *The Crying of Lot 49*" by John Hunt. From *Critical Essays on Thomas Pynchon* edited by Richard Pearce (Boston: G.K. Hall & Co., 1981): pp. 32, 38–41. © 1981 by G.K. Hall & Co. Reprinted by permission of The Gale Group.

"*The Crying of Lot 49*" by Tony Tanner. From *Thomas Pynchon* (London: Methuen, 1982): pp. 56–57, 66–67, 71–73. © 1982 by Tony Tanner. Reprinted by permission.

"Finding *V.*" by Kenneth Kupsch. From *Twentieth Century Literature: A Scholarly and Critical Journal* 44, no. 4 (1998): p. 428–31, 444–45. © 1999 by Hofstra University. Reprinted by permission.

"The Politics of Literary Reinscription in Thomas Pynchon's *V.*" by Mark Sanders. From *Critique: Studies in Contemporary Fiction* 39, no. 1 (1997): p. 81–82, 95. Reprinted with permission of the Helen Dwight Reid Educational Foundation. Published by Heldref Publications, 1319 Eighteenth St., NW, Washington, DC 20036-1802. Copyright © 1997.

"A 'Hermaphrodite Sort of Deity': Sexuality, Gender, and Gender Blending in Thomas Pynchon's *V.*" by Mark D. Hawthorne. From *Studies in the Novel* 29, no. 1 (1997): p. 74–76. © 1997 by Mark D. Hawthorne. Reprinted by permission.

"Profaned and Stenciled Texts: In Search of Pynchon's *V.*" by Melvyn New. From *Thomas Pynchon: Modern Critical Views*, edited by Harold Bloom (New York: Chelsea House, 1986): pp. 97–98, 99, 102. © 1986 by Melvyn New. Reprinted by permission of the author.

"Vacillating in the Void? Verbal Vivication in *V.*" by Deborah L. Madsen. From *The Postmodernist Allegories of Thomas Pynchon* (1991): pp. 29–30, 50–52. © 1991 by Deborah L. Madsen. Reprinted by permission of the author.

"What is Thomas Pynchon Telling Us?" by Josephine Hendin. From *Harpers* 250 no. 1498 (March, 1975): pp. 37–39. © 1975 by Josephine Hendin. Reprinted by permission.

"'Making the Unreal Reel': Film in *Gravity's Rainbow*" from *Thomas Pynchon: The Art of Allusion* by David Cowart. (Southern Illinois UP, 1980): pp. 31–32, 33–35, 60–62. © 1980 by Southern Illinois University Press, reprinted by permission of the publisher.

"Looking Back on Sodom: Sixties Sadomasochism in *Gravity's Rainbow*" by John Hamill. From *Critique: Studies in Contemporary Fiction* 41, no. 1 (1999): p. 53, 68–69. © 1999 by Heldref. Reprinted with permission of the Helen Dwight Reid Educational Foundation. Published by Heldref Publications, 1319 Eighteenth St., NW, Washington DC 20036-1802. Copyright © 1999.

"Amerikkka Uber Alles: German Nationalism, American Imperialism, and the 1960s Antiwar Movement in *Gravity's Rainbow*" by Jeffrey S. Baker. From *Critique: Studies in Contemporary Fiction* 40, no. 4 (1999): p. 323–25, 339–340. © 1999 by Heldref. Reprinted with permission of the Helen Dwight Reid Educational Foundation. Published by Heldref Publications, 1319 Eighteenth St., NW, Washington, DC 20036-1802. Copyright © 1999.

"Gravity's Encyclopedia" by Edward Mendelson. From *Mindful Pleasures: Essays On Thomas Pynchon* edited by George Levine and

David Leverenz, (Boston: Little, Brown and Company, 1976): pp. 161, 171–173, 191–92. © 1976 by Edward Mendelson. Reprinted by permission of the author.

"Creative Paranoia and Frost Patterns of White Words" by Gabriele Schwab. From *Thomas Pynchon's Gravity's Rainbow*, edited by Harold Bloom (New York: Chelsea House, 1986): pp. 108–110. © 1986 by Chelsea House Publishers. Reprinted by permission.

"Science and Technology" by John O. Stark. From *Pynchon's Fictions: Thomas Pynchon and the Literature of Information*. Athens: Ohio University Press, 1980, pp. 45–49, 73. © 1980 by Ohio State University Press. Reprinted by permission of the Ohio State University Press.

"Sari, Sorry, and the Vortex of History: Calendar Reform, Anachronism, and Language Change in *Mason & Dixon*" by Elizabeth Jane Wall Hinds. From *American Literary History* 12, no. 1–2 (2000): p. 206–209. © 2000 by Elizabeth Jane Wall Hinds. Reprinted by permission of the author.

"The Luddite Vision: *Mason & Dixon*" by David Cowart. From *American Literature: A Journal of Literary History, Criticism, and Bibliography* 71, no. 2 (1999): p. 341–43, 362–63. © 1999 by David Cowart. Reprinted by permission.

"Cognitive and Pragmatic Linguistic Moments: Literary Epiphany in Thomas Pynchon and Seamus Heaney" by Ashton Nichols. From *Moments of Moment: Aspects of the Literary Epiphany* edited by Wim Tigges (Amsterdam: Rodopi BV, 1999) p. 468–69, 475–77, 479–80. © 1999 by Rodopi. Reprinted by permission.

"Pynchon in the Poetic" by William Logan. From *Southwest Review* 83 no. 4 (Southern Methodist University, 1998) pp. 424–26, 435–37. © 1998 by William Logan. Reprinted by permission.

"Separation and Linkage in Pynchon's *Mason & Dixon*" by William McCarron. From *Notes on Contemporary Literature* 28, 1 : 1998. pp. 12–14. © 1998 by William McCarron. Reprinted by permission.

"Lightness and Gravity: Calvino, Pynchon, and Postmodernity" by Alessia Ricciardi. From *MLN* 114, 5 (1999): pp. 1062, 1065–66, 1071–72. © 1999 by Alessia Ricciardi. Reprinted by permission.

INDEX OF
Themes and Ideas

CRYING OF LOT 49, THE, 12, 91, 98–99, 127–29, 133, 138; ambiguity in, 28–32; characters in, 21–22; Genghis Cohen in, 18–19, 22, 36; comedy in, 36–41; critical views on, 23–46; Randoph Driblette in, 17, 19, 22; Mike Fallopian in, 16–17, 21, 35; function of entropy in, 41–46; Doctor Hilarius in, 19, 21–22, 34, 39; Pierce Inverarity in, 15–17, 21, 35–36, 38–39, 42–43; Mucho Maas in, 15–16, 19, 21–22, 34; Oedipa Maas in, 15–28, 37–46, 91, 99, 128; Oedipa's paranoia in, 33–36; Metzger in, 15–17, 19, 21–22, 39, 128; Miles in, 15, 22; John Nefastis in, 18, 22, 43–44; numerous codes in, 26–27; plot summary of, 15–20; Roseman in, 15, 22; science and technology in, 23–25

"ENTROPY," 12, 70, 98–100

GRAVITY'S RAINBOW, 13, 54–55, 59, 63–65, 67, 79, 126–29, 145; Seaman Bodine in, 85–86, 90, 104, 145; Katje Borgesius in, 83–84, 86–87, 89, 112; characters in, 88–90; critical views on, 91–115; encyclopedic nature in, 103–6; Oberst Enzian in, 87, 89, 112; Bianca Erdmann in, 86, 90; Margherita ("Greta") Erdmann in, 85–86, 90, 93–95; Gottfried in, 83, 87, 89–90; implications of film and cinema in, 91–95; Lazlo Jamf in, 82, 84, 88, 113; Roger Mexico in, 82, 84, 87–88, 104; plot summary of, 81–87; Dr. Edward W.A. ("Ned") Pointsman in, 82, 84, 86–90; politics of America in the sixties in, 97–102; Geoffrey "Pirate" Prentice in, 81–83, 86–89; Ernest Pudding in, 82–83, 86, 89, 96, 104; rebirth and hope in, 106–10; role of sadomasochism in, 95–97; science and technology in, 110–15; Tyrone Slothrop in, 82–90, 92–95, 104–5, 112–13; Jessica Swanlake in, 82, 87–88, 90; Vaslav Tchitcherine in, 85–86, 89–90; Geli Tripping in, 85, 90; Blodget Waxwing in, 84, 90; Captain/Major Weissmann (Blicero) in, 83, 89–90, 97, 112

"IS IT O.K. TO BE A LUDDITE?," 13

"A JOURNEY INTO THE MIND OF WATTS," 13

"LOWLANDS," 12

MASON & DIXON, 13, 54, 90; Armand Allègre in, 118, 121; anachronism in, 124–28; Fender-Belly Bodine in, 121, 145; characters in, 121–23; Reverend Wicks Cherrycoke in, 116–22, 138, 145–46; conflict between rationality and spirituality in, 128–33; critical views on, 124–49; Jeremiah Dixon in, 116–17, 119–26, 130, 132, 135, 140, 142–44, 146–48; epiphanies in, 133–37; experimental postmodernity in, 145–49; Fang or the Learned English Dog in, 117, 121–22, 144; Dr. Benjamin Franklin in, 117, 119, 122, 127, 130–31, 142, 145; Elizabeth LeSpark in, 122; John LeSpark in, 116–17, 122; Pitt LeSpark in, 116, 119, 122; Pliny LeSpark in, 116, 119, 122; Tenebrae LeSpark in, 116, 122; Reverend Dr. Nevil Maskelyne in, 122; Charles Mason in, 116–26, 128, 130, 132, 135, 140, 142–44, 146–48; Mary Mason in, 122; Rebekah Mason in, 117, 122, 128; plot summary of, 116–20; poetic tendencies in, 138–42; theme of separation and linkage in, 143–45; "Vaucanson's Mechanickal Duck" in, 118, 121, 144; Professor Voam in, 118, 122; the Vroom family in, 123; Cornelius Vroom in, 122; Colonel George Washington in, 118, 123, 130–31, 142, 145–46; Father Zarpazo in, 118, 123, 142; Captain/Doctor Zhang in, 118, 123, 142

"MORTALITY AND MERCY IN VIENNA," 12

PYNCHON, THOMAS, biography of, 12–14; works about, 151–54; works by, 150

SLOW LEARNER, 13, 98

"UNDER THE ROSE," 12

V., 12, 14, 24, 37–39, 81, 83, 85, 90–91, 114, 129; alternative historical events in, 62–65; Pig Bodine in, 47, 54, 121; characters in, 53–56; critical views on, 57; Dudley Eigenvalue in, 49, 56; figure of death in, 76–80; gender roles in, 65–68; Evan Godolphin in, 48–49, 51, 55–56, 71; Hugh Godolphin in, 55, 61, 72; Mr. Goodfellow in, 55; Esther Harvitz in, 48, 56; Carla Maijstral in, 55; Junior Fausto Maijstral in, 55; Senior Fausto Maijstral in, 50–51, 55, 58, 67; Paola Maijstral in, 47, 50, 53–56; Angel Mendoza, 55; Josefina Mendoza in, 49, 53, 55; Kurt Mondaugen in, 49–50, 55, 64–65; Rachel Owlglass in, 47, 53–54, 56; plot summary of, 47–52; process of criticism on, 68–71; Benny Profane in, 47–51, 53–55, 60–62, 67–68, 70, 77–79; Shale Schoenmaker in, 48, 56; Herbert Stencil in, 39–40, 47–55, 58–60, 62, 66–70, 73–74; Sidney Stencil in, 48, 51, 53, 55, 73, 75; V. in, 47–56, 66–69, 71, 78–79; V.'s elusiveness in, 71–76; the true identity of V. in, 57–62; The Whole Sick Crew in, 47–48, 54, 70, 114

VINELAND, 13, 99, 129, 138